MW00388273

PLANT-BASED
USA

PLANT-BASED USA

A TRAVEL GUIDE TO EATING ANIMAL-FREE IN AMERICA

VERONICA FIL

Hardie Grant

EXPLORE

INTRODUCTION

Australia was burning, with wildfires tearing through the country at a rate we'd never seen before. News reports had started to emerge about this weird flu spreading across the world. I'd been binge-watching *Love Is Blind* on Netflix as all the signs of an impending apocalypse loomed in the air. And among it all, my husband and I were in the process of packing up our lives in Melbourne and moving to Los Angeles, the other side of the world, to launch our plant-based food startup.

That's the scene I remember in February 2020, when the team at Hardie Grant Explore first contacted me and asked if I'd like to write a book, a travel guide for plant-based dining. Of course, I leapt at the opportunity. I had never been more busy in my life, but this was not something I was willing to pass up.

A few weeks later, something happened that none of us expected. The world literally shut down. We'd heard murmurings about a new megavirus for weeks, but this was *28 Days Later*-level. The streets went silent; stores sealed up; basic necessities like toilet paper were stripped from the shelves. International borders closed. And restaurants, unsure of what this all meant, were forced to close indefinitely.

At the time, we thought it might only last a few weeks, then everything would settle back to normal. No normal came. There was no relief, just confusion, horrifying news broadcasts about the climbing death toll, and a rising sense of paranoia and fear. Food service providers were given little direction or clarity around the rules. Was outdoor dining acceptable? Did the customers need masks? Were restaurants even allowed to be open each day? While some were able to pivot quickly to an online delivery model, others lacked the resources to stay afloat. The death toll grew further, and it wasn't just taking human lives but small businesses too.

That's when the purpose of this book changed. It became less about romping through restaurants and discovering the best in plant-based cuisine. Instead, I wanted to focus on the people who are pushing the future of food forward and building a system that no longer relies on animal consumption. It's about the founders, chefs, entrepreneurs, and brands that are all committed to change.

For transparency, the venues and brands featured throughout his book are not being rated, ranked, or even reviewed. All opinions are my own (and when it comes to food, those opinions can be arbitrary). They've each been selected because, regardless of my personal tastes, they're doing something special while displacing animals from the food system in the process.

I hope these pages come in handy when you're in search of your next meal.

ACKNOWLEDGMENTS

Thank you to the chefs, restaurateurs, founders, and business owners who contributed to this book and the progress of the plant-based dining scene.

An extra special thank you to the team members of Grounded Foods Co.—Justin Wilkin, Connor Daniel, Robert Brady, and Shana Ostroweicki—who helped me in my research or simply took pressure out of my schedule so I could focus.

And of course, thank you to my astonishingly talented, unwaveringly focused, and relentlessly loving husband, Shaun Quade, who is the inspiration behind my business and the content of this book.

GLOSSARY

ANIMAL-FREE

Any food that does not come directly from an animal source

CELL-BASED MEAT, CULTURED MEAT, OR CULTIVATED MEAT

Real meat derived from cultivated animal stem cells that eliminates the need to raise animals for livestock

OMNI

Short for *omnivore*, a diet consisting of both animals and plants

PLANT-BASED

For the purposes of this book, I use the term "plant-based" to describe any foods that do not contain any animal-derived ingredients. It is used interchangeably with the word *vegan*.

PLANT-FORWARD

Reduced consumption/usage of animal-derived ingredients in favor of plants

SEITAN

A meat substitute made from wheat gluten

TEXTURED VEGETABLE PROTEIN (TVP)

A traditional meat substitute made from defatted soy flour

VEGAN

A person who does not eat any food derived from animals and who typically avoids animal products in their lifestyle (including clothing)

ON THE PAGE

The book has been divided up into major cities across the country; however there are a few noteworthy national chains I've highlighted in the Other Venues section (*see* p. 256), as well as several exceptional vegan delis dotted across the country (*see* p. 250).

Under each business heading, I've noted if a place is purely vegan, vegetarian, or has vegan options available. I've also highlighted any woman-owned or black-owned businesses, to help support those doing interesting things in the plant-based space. I've included some great Q+As with other plant-based entrepreneurs, to discuss their secrets, tips, some of the challenges they face, and generally celebrate animal-free eating.

CITIES

NTA
NTA
NTA
NTA
NTA

The city of Atlanta, Georgia, isn't famous for its thriving food scene. At least, not in the same way that Chicago is known for its heavy slabs of deep dish pizza and California is the embodiment of a juice cleanse. But in typical Southern tradition, its most iconic dishes involve BBQ meats and fried chicken, making Atlanta a difficult city to navigate if you're of the plant-forward persuasion. Difficult, but not impossible.

Atlanta's dining culture took flight, so to speak, in the 1960s when Delta Airlines added a nonstop route to the city from California. This opened it up to an influx of ethnic cuisines, ingredients, and cooking methods, which are still represented today in a diverse mix of restaurants.

While Southern comfort food dominates most menus and home kitchens, in summertime Atlanta becomes a candyland for fresh, U-Pick produce—from blueberries, strawberries, and apples to plump Georgia peaches. It also scores high on farmers' markets; you're likely to find at least one operating any day of the week.

I recommend the eclectic **Dekalb Farmers Market** as a starting point. It's been around since the 1970s and is a solid all-rounder for fresh produce. For the purposes of this book, be sure to skip the overwhelming meat and dairy sections; you've got no business there.

Mass consumption and waste is a personal peeve of mine, so I love the concept behind **World Market Recycling**, a community center located at the Dekalb Farmers Market where members of the public can haul their junk to save it from landfill and learn more about how to recycle properly in the process. Because let's be honest: recycling is way more complicated than it needs to be. Every city differs in terms of what it will and won't accept; your mascara tube can be recycled but the wand cannot; your spray bottle of all-purpose cleaner can be recycled but not the squirting nozzle; and we're all still thoroughly confused about the status of greasy pizza boxes. At World Market Recycling, they'll help break down the rules so you can stop wondering. Plus, if you arrive early, you might score a few treasures that deserve a second life.

For everyday groceries, try **Sevananda Natural Foods Market**, one of only four vegan/vegetarian co-op grocers in the country. Here, you can buy everything a conventional store would stock, apart from meat and seafood, and they don't accept products that have artificial, GMO, irradiated, or animal ingredients. There's also an impressive bulk department. You'll need a membership to shop there, but the signup is quick and can be done either in-store or online.

ATLANTA

DEKALB FARMERS MARKET +
WORLD MARKET RECYCLING
3000 E Ponce De Leon Avenue
Decatur, GA 30030

SEVANANDA NATURAL
FOODS MARKET
467 Moreland Avenue NE
Atlanta, GA 30307

SLUTTY VEGAN

VEGAN | WOMAN-OWNED

→ **1542 RALPH DAVID ABERNATHY BOULEVARD SW
ATLANTA, GA 30310**

→ **164 N MCDONOUGH STREET
JONESBORO, GA 30236**

→ **476 EDGEWOOD AVENUE SE
ATLANTA, GA 30312**

If you haven't heard of Slutty Vegan before, you're probably not vegan. This fast-food concept is notorious for its party atmosphere, sassy voice, and contribution to plant-based publicity. What started in 2018 as a food truck has grown to become an example of brilliant business acumen as well as a source of endless provocation to those suffering from word sensitivities.

The menu is worth a look-see for the names alone: Slut Sauce, Super Slut, Hollywood Hooker. I don't know how they get away with it in today's PC culture, but they do. And before you pull out the old quill and ink to pen an angry letter, Google the name Pinky Cole. She's the superstar entrepreneur who's not only built a small burger empire, but has inspired an entire legion of young aspiring business owners to go get it. When Cole isn't busy growing her fleet of eateries, she's working on the Pinky Cole Foundation to support economic progress and business leadership in the Black community.

The burgers are pretty pricey for Atlanta standards, ranging anywhere from $15 to $19, but they come loaded with ingredients like guacamole, jalapeños, vegan cheese, caramelized onions, lettuce, tomato, vegan beef patties, bacon, or shrimp. And they all include fries on the side (obviously these are served with a sprinkle of Slut Dust, which I think refers to flavored salt, but I could be wrong).

Coming here is like an event. It's not unusual to walk up and find the line out the door, with celebrities live-streaming to their socials to prove they were there. But if none of that matters to you, visit for the sheer fact that the food tastes really damn good. After all, going vegan doesn't mean you can't still have a bit of fun.

LOV'N IT LIVE

VEGAN

→ **2796 E POINT STREET
EAST POINT, GA 30344**

First, a confession: it's been a couple of decades since I last ate nutmeat. Mom used to cook with it all the time; it was the feature of weeknight stroganoffs and meatloafs, and I never once complained. I loved the stuff. That was until the day I saw it come out of a tin—bearing an unmistakable resemblance to cheap dog food—and from that point on, I refused to put it in my mouth.

Now, I don't know if it's because my palate has matured since then or if it's simply the result of skilled kitchen preparation, but I have to say that I'm back in the nutmeat game. These dense, meaty cubes of protein feature heavily on the Lov'n It Live menu and have triggered a whole new appreciation for the 1980s vegetarian staple. Their kitchen team uses it in nori rolls, stuffed avocado, cabbage tacos, burgers, sandwiches, and pretty much anywhere meat is normally found. I honestly find nutmeat just as satisfying as any other meat substitute, even at a time when hyper-real, lab-grown meat is getting investors all hot and bothered like the next dot-com boom.

The team at Lov'n It Live don't just talk the talk; they follow through with nutrient-rich ingredients, an understanding of how diet affects our well-being, and a genuine sense of care and consideration in every dish. Today, that message is being expressed through lentil burgers, raw vegetables, carob brownies, and the aforementioned nutmeat because not all meat and dairy alternatives need to be made in a Silicon Valley bioreactor to be exciting.

HERBAN FIX

VEGAN

→ **565-A PEACHTREE STREET NE
ATLANTA, GA 30308**

Having operated restaurants for almost four decades, Chef Wendy
Chang is considered a hospitality legend. Originally from Taiwan,
she specializes in cooking healthy pan-Asian cuisine as a cultural
expression of her heritage and American home.

More recently, her skills have been channeled into the thoughtful
dining experience that is Herban Fix. While the menu is hard
to define, it centers around fresh, seasonal ingredients and creative
reinterpretations of classic Asian dishes. Don't expect to find sweet
and sour chicken on the menu; it's not P.F. Chang's. Instead, diners
are spoiled with beautifully balanced bowls of ja jiang buckwheat
noodles tossed with Asian pear and cucumber and pan-seared soy
fish with organic kale simmered in a light curry laksa that almost
makes you feel healthier just for ordering it.

"Fusion" style cooking is heavily referenced at Herban Fix,
and it's nowhere more evident than in dishes like the spinach
and mushroom ravioli in curry jus with edamame or the organic
white bean and pumpkin bouillon with pine nuts, which both lean
more clearly toward a Western palate. I know the word *fusion* gets
scoffed at by chefs these days, but I think it still has its place as an
effective descriptor. So I say go for it. Do the fusion. Live your truth.

I admit that, while Herban Fix isn't aiming to achieve the whole
stuffy fine-dining aesthetic, it does have the kind of upmarket
feel that makes you want to consult the price of each dish first.
And that's OK because this isn't a restaurant you patronize when
you want a quick and dirty meal. It's a place to chill out and enjoy
the atmosphere. Or conduct an intense interview of your vegan
Bumble date without the hectic clatter of the local food court
to distract you.

I'd happily take a nonvegan date here and feel confident that
they wouldn't complain about the lack of meat during the Uber
ride home. The dishes are delicious. They might, however, take
issue with the small portion sizes and price and ask to stop by
Burger King on the way back, in which case ... swipe left. It's
a good excuse to come back again with someone else.

BOLE ETHIOPIAN RESTAURANT

VEGAN OPTIONS AVAILABLE

→ **1583 VIRGINIA AVENUE
COLLEGE PARK, GA 30337**

Bole Ethiopian isn't exclusively vegan or vegetarian, but the family that runs it is so passionate about sharing their culture through food and good hospitality that it deserves to be featured among these pages.

If you're easily triggered by a kitchen that cooks with egg or shrimp, this isn't the place for you. But those who can live with that will find the vegan options easy to navigate, plentiful, and abundant in flavor.

The veggie platter comes with the obligatory bed of injera (a cross between flatbread and a pancake), which is specifically designed to be dipped into the rich sauces that Ethiopian cuisine is known for. It's then adorned with shiro; lentil and chickpea stew; cabbage, potatoes, and carrots; Ethiopian-style collard greens; and a green bean and carrot stir-fry.

There's also a small section of "fusion" style pasta dishes that come in vegetarian and vegan options. My advice would be to stick with the combination plates so you can sample a bit of everything. There's enough variety that you won't miss the meaty bits. And don't be surprised if your nonvegan dining companions hog the veggie dishes; in fact, it might be best to order extra.

I've always thought of Los Angeles as the national capital of clean eating, but a couple of years ago, Austin made its way onto my radar as the unlikely Texan hotspot for plant-based foodies and alternative living.

Case in point: Austin is the birthplace of **Whole Foods**, the best-known natural grocer in the country and the place every food entrepreneur dreams of getting their products stocked. If, like me, you find the prospect of touring grocery stores in various cities thrilling, then head to their flagship megastore on North Lamar Boulevard. There's almond milk, nut butter, and organic kale chips up the wazoo.

But be warned: Austin is not a quiet city. Music flows everywhere, from beer gardens and backyard raves to buskers playing outside the local grocery store. It's also the home of **South by Southwest (SXSW)**, the internationally renowned and all-encompassing creative festival that takes over the city for ten days each year. Every March, thousands of people from all over the world flock to the city to take part in the event's TED Talk–like conference sessions and music, film, comedy, and art festival showcases.

For something a little more chill, whip out your bathing suit and head to **Barton Springs**. This popular state parkland features a glorious natural pool that's safe for public swimming so long as you look out for the local wildlife. Visitors can paddle alongside turtles and fish, including Austin's beloved native salamander. It costs a few dollars to get in, but it makes for a relaxing and affordable way to beat the heat.

WHOLE FOODS FLAGSHIP STORE
525 N Lamar Boulevard
Austin, TX 78703

BARTON SPRINGS
2201 William Barton Drive
Austin, TX 78746

SXSW
sxsw.com

REBEL CHEESE

VEGAN

→ **2200 ALDRICH STREET, SUITE 120
AUSTIN, TX 78723**

I spent a lot of time in wine bars throughout my twenties. I'd like to say it was a reflection of my thriving dating life, but no. In reality, it was just me enjoying a few glasses of red and immersing myself in fine cheeses while I penned my latest manuscript. I look back on those times fondly because, as a startup founder, I rarely get the time to leave my desk anymore, let alone swirl wine around in my glass as I gaze thoughtfully into the distance.

But that's why I was delighted to discover vegan deli and wine bar Rebel Cheese. It's run by Kirsten Maitland and Fred Zwar, who make their range of artisan-style cheeses by hand using cashews and traditional fermentation methods.

Those who can't make it to their Austin location in person can subscribe to the monthly Rebel Cheese Club, which summons a box of exquisitely packaged cheeses directly to your door. The selections are constantly changing but might include a chèvre, Brie, pepperjack, cheddar, or something special from Rebel's development kitchen.

The wine bar/deli also offers a range of plant-based charcuterie plates, sandwiches, soups, and salads, which also serve as excellent vehicles for cheese delivery.

TIP

Rebel Cheese does catering, so if you're in town for an event, be sure to steer the organizers their way.

COUNTER CULTURE

VEGAN

→ **2337 E CESAR CHAVEZ STREET
AUSTIN, TX 78702**

In 2009, Chef Sue Davis started Counter Culture as a food truck with a goal to provide the people of Austin with healthier, more affordable food while reducing their environmental footprint. The concept quickly took off—so much so that, by 2012, Sue had sold the wheels and moved to a more permanent brick-and-mortar location.

Counter Culture's animal-free and raw-food menu is made from scratch using local and organic ingredients wherever possible. There's nothing mass-produced going on here, unlike some unmentionable fast-food chains (who can keep their suspicious tubs of slimy burger sauce that have a six-year shelf life). Instead, Counter Culture delivers house-made seitan, cheeses, sauces, ketchup, and yogurt straight into your mouth hole. Anything that's not made on the premises, such as kombucha, tempeh, and ice cream, is sourced from local and independent farmers.

Keep this place on your list if you're into natural, unprocessed foods and ingredients you can actually pronounce.

MR. NATURAL

VEGAN

→ **1901 E CESAR CHAVEZ STREET
AUSTIN, TX 78702**

→ **2414A S LAMAR BOULEVARD
AUSTIN, TX 78704**

Mr. Natural health food store and bakery is the embodiment
of one of those vintage vegetarian cookbooks you can score in
thrift stores (if you're lucky). Its retro decor and focus on whole-
food ingredients tell a story of a simpler time, when companies
making soy burgers weren't positioning themselves as the next
Tesla. Makes sense, considering Mr. Natural's been operating
since 1988.

Back then, founders Jesus and Maria set out to build a place
to nurture both the mind and mouth using holistic practices. The
store, which has since expanded into baked goods and restaurant
meals, now spans two locations that are managed by the
couple's children.

Stop by for cakes, pies, pastries, and a kaleidoscope of baked
goods—including sugar-free and spelt options—or stock up
on supplements.

THE BEER PLANT

VEGAN

→ **3110 WINDSOR ROAD**
AUSTIN, TX 78703

Any time I hear the word *gastropub*, I think of a town called Fitzroy in Australia. It's an eclectic area populated by young creatives, students, and a dab of wealthy Gen Xers living in multimillion-dollar, graffitied warehouse conversions. The number of bars, pubs, and restaurants lining Fitzroy's streets seem to outweigh its population.

I miss my days sitting at those pub benches in the sun. I'd be there all dressed up, tapping at my keyboard and drinking cider, waiting for one of the local, hapless, chain-smoking, but typically very good-looking musicians to notice me. Ah, memories. Since moving to the US, I've struggled to find a new local spot where I could relive that experience, but now I understand that this problem could have been easily rectified had I only visited Austin sooner. That's where I found The Beer Plant and its entirely plant-based menu.

Menu-wise, they've got all of the standard staples, from buffalo cauliflower wings and loaded fries to mac and cheese and other delectables. But as you delve deeper into the menu, things start to get interesting with dishes like the Nashville hot and crispy, which is comprised of a crunchy mound of battered king oyster mushrooms, pickled celery, purple cabbage, and remoulade on a pretzel bun. In my opinion, the use of remoulade immediately elevates any venue to a higher level of gastronomical experience.

The menu here changes quite frequently, but because it's all vegan, there's no guesswork required. If you do have additional concerns about The Beer Plant's ingredients, the staff can provide an extensive allergen guide detailing exactly what's in each dish. That kind of attention to detail is what good hospitality is all about.

BOULDIN CREEK CAFE

VEGETARIAN | VEGAN OPTIONS AVAILABLE

→ **1900 S FIRST STREET
AUSTIN, TX 78704**

There's something satisfyingly nostalgic about the Bouldin Creek Cafe website, especially if you're old enough to have had a Myspace account. It offers a sense of comfort that carries all the way through to their menu, which reads like one from an unusually wholesome roadside diner that your mom has somehow taken over the kitchen of.

Expect to find traditional breakfasts, sandwiches, and "big azz" salads (their words, not mine) day and night. A few things make this eatery stand out from the pack. Firstly, everything comes with a solid vegan option, so if the organic free-range eggs don't tickle your fancy, there's always a tofu substitute to leave you equally satisfied. Secondly, dishes are prepared simply and transparently, using mostly unprocessed ingredients instead of prepackaged mock meats.

There's a definite bohemian vibe going on at Bouldin Creek Cafe; colorful walls are plastered with paintings and stickers, the stools don't quite match, and the place is punctuated by the odd disco ball and fixie bike. I'd feel just as comfortable coming here alone for a coffee to write my memoirs as I would with a group of friends for Sunday mimosas. There would be a family digging into a juicy plate of tacos on one side, a collective of students discussing the nuances of David Foster Wallace's catalog of work on the other, and we'd all, in that moment, be connected by a mutual appreciation of tofu.

THE VEGAN NOM

VEGAN

→ **2324 E CESAR CHAVEZ STREET AUSTIN, TX 78702**

As their website proudly states, The Vegan Nom is "Austin's original vegan taco truck in Austin, Texas," and I'd have to agree. But also The Vegan Nom might be Austin's most original taco truck full stop, vegan or not.

Chris Rios's transportable vegan van has weathered the distance in a city known for its carnivorous tendencies. His entrepreneurial journey started in 2011, when he worked out of an old Airstream, assembling tacos with his range of secret signature sauces that touted maximum flavor, zero animal byproducts, and no nuts. The locals were quick to get on board.

Since then, Chris has expanded The Vegan Nom's concept into three outposts, all sporting bigger trucks and broader menus that feature burritos, nachos, and a breakfast selection. Ingredients are far from traditional; options include Korean BBQ, buffalo chicken, and tempeh bacon and scrambled tofu burritos. You can also take home your own packet of Planet Queso cheese mix, a nut-free dairy alternative made with legumes that was created specifically for The Vegan Nom's menu.

CASA DE LUZ

VEGAN

→ **1701 TOOMEY ROAD
AUSTIN, TX 78704**

Nestled among the deep-green leaves of hanging vines, Casa de Luz is not so much a restaurant but a destination for those seeking nourishment of the body and mind. Visitors come here for workshops, classes, and events that support mindfulness and healing, but also for the fixed-price menu, which changes daily and centers around organic, wholesome, and macrobiotic ingredients. Don't expect to find any battered soy nugs, but do expect hearty salads, curries, leafy greens, pickled vegetables, soups, freshly made tortillas, and whole grains (which are presoaked to assist in the digestive process).

In addition to being 100% vegan, Casa de Luz prepares meals in accordance with a gluten-free, refined oil–free, and refined sugar–free philosophy. Furthermore, all ingredients are organic, meaning they're free from pesticides and chemical growth enhancers (aka they're laying off the 'roids).

The space is situated alongside the local Montessori school, with a nonprofit farm called Casa del Sol operating behind the restaurant itself. Interestingly, the farm works on the principles of agroecology, which is a sustainable agricultural practice that aims to find balance between animals, plants, and the ecosystem surrounding us. More of that, please.

BOULDIN CREEK CAFE (*see* p. 18)

REBEL CHEESE (*see* p. 14)

COUNTER CULTURE (*see* p. 15)

CHICAGO

Don't be dissuaded by Chicago's affinity for lard-laden deep dish pizza or the fact that it has historically served as the headquarters of the meatpacking industry. This city still has a vibrant community of plant-based enthusiasts. In fact, you might say that America's entire vegetarian movement originated in Chicago (well, the state of Illinois to be more accurate).

It all started back in 1893, when the country's first ever vegetarian society was established in Chicago. They didn't have Impossible patties back then, but they did have fertile and flat farmland, which, to this day, makes an ideal environment for cultivating soybeans and corn. If you want to learn more about Chicago's animal-free history, you're in luck; the city just so happens to be home to the one and only national **Vegan Museum**, a traveling roadshow that pops up in a new location every couple of months. You can track down its latest whereabouts by visiting veganmuseum.org.

I have a special affinity for Chicago's food scene. Since 2016, I've been coming here every year for the **National Restaurant Association Show** (which the event organizers continue to refer to as the NRA Show despite the problematic optics), along with thousands of chefs, restaurant owners, hospitality pros, and food brands.

The first time I attended the show in 2016, I noticed a large booth that stood out from the rows of dairy and hotdog-tasting stations. It was branded as "Beyond Meat," and it beckoned me to sample a "plant burger that tastes just like the real thing." People were circling the booth with suspicion, but I dove straight in for a taste; after all, I was raised by a lentil-loving momma, so I have no fear of threatening vegan meat alternatives. And from the moment I took a bite, I was sold. I'd never tried a plant-based burger that was so spot on in flavor and texture.

As I continued to roam through the massive pavilions, I came across another booth, this time demonstrating a sushi alternative made from tomato flesh. Again, it was delicious. I was so incredibly excited by these meat and seafood alternatives, not because they were vegan or more sustainable, but because they were novel and simply tasted good.

That was the moment I knew plant-based food was about to take off. When I got home from that trip, it struck me that nobody was making dairy-free cheese at the same level. The entire category seemed to have missed out on the innovations. So I mentioned it to my chef-husband Shaun and told him we should develop a plant-based cheese that everyday people would happily eat without noticing it didn't contain dairy. "Massive market opportunity," I said. "We'd be millionaires." Alas, he shrugged it off at the time and argued that nobody wanted vegan cheese.

I guess Shaun had a change of mind. Because here we are a few years later as the founders of one of the most wildly innovative plant-based cheese companies in the world. And it all started with a visit to Chicago.

We're far from being millionaires, but you know ... there's still time.

AMITABUL

VEGAN

→ **6207 N MILWAUKEE AVENUE
CHICAGO, IL 60646**

Bill Choi wasn't always like this. Years ago, after leaving his hometown in Seoul, South Korea, Bill found himself working at a run-of-the-mill Chicago grill, spending his days flipping eggs and burgers. It was during that time that the monks from his local Buddhist temple would visit, laden with fresh vegetables. He'd use the produce to make bi bim bop (also known as bibimbap), a Korean dish of rice topped with mixed vegetables.

According to Bill, the success of this impromptu menu item inspired him to open a restaurant of his own, now known as Amitabul, only his would be plant-forward and shy away from added oils and salts. Back in 1995—a time when deep dish pizza and greasy Chicago diner grub governed the city—this was a radical concept, but after thirty years, Amitabul has truly carved out its place in the city's dining scene and, with it, a reputation for thoughtful, flavor-filled Korean cuisine prepared with genuine care.

The OG bi bim bop dish remains on the menu too.

ALTHEA

VEGAN

→ **700 N MICHIGAN AVENUE, 7TH FLOOR CHICAGO, IL 60611**

Imagine you're shopping at Saks Fifth Avenue downtown when you find yourself weary from several hours of shopping and lugging the immense weight of all your new Balenciaga handbags and Blahnik shoes (I wish). Your chauffeur is late, and you simply can't deal without having a bite to eat of something Instagrammable. That's when Chef Matthew Kenney enters the chat with Althea, his high-end dining concept located within the infamous Saks shopping mecca itself.

It's the perfect fit for a fashion destination. Gorgeous plates of avocado toast delicately topped with tahini, preserved lemon, watermelon radish, serrano peppers, and pea shoots are almost too pretty for some influencers to actually eat. Not me; I'm devouring it. Althea offers a walk on the light side, with fresh, flavorful, and raw dishes being the only options. One of the heartiest dishes is a kelp noodle cacio e pepe, which is arguably a snack in my opinion, but nevertheless provides a creative and better-for-you spin on the traditional, cream-laden pasta dish. Served with lush, peppery cashew cream; sugar snap peas; and crispy olives, it's just enough to tide you over until you're ready to hit the luxury bath towels section.

5 MINUTES WITH

CHLOE MENDEL

**FASHION DESIGNER AND CO-OWNER OF
MADAME ZUZU'S EMPORIUM**

Chloe comes from a lineage of furriers, and is the sixth generation of the House of Mendel designers. However, she's the first to deploy her talents through the creation of a luxury faux fur brand, Maison Atia. Chloe also runs Madame ZuZu's Emporium alongside her partner, Billy Corgan (of Smashing Pumpkins). Their multipurpose venue is part tea house, part cafe, and part event space, and sells a curated collection of books and vinyl records. There's lots to explore here, and it's well worth a visit if you're near Highland Park.

→ **Tell us about Maison Atia and what drew you to create a sustainable fashion brand.**

Maison Atia is a brand that was born out of the values and passions I have today for sustainability while still celebrating my family history and tradition.

I come from a lineage of furriers and am sixth generation of the Mendel family. While working in my father's atelier, I would always think, "Why isn't there faux fur that I would want to buy? Why can't faux furs be made with the same attention to detail like the real thing?" Thus, Maison Atia was born!

In this century, it was equally important to me to have a brand that was charitable (we rescue a homeless pet with each coat sold), transparent, and sustainable. We launched in 2017, and soon after that, many other luxury brands decided to go "fur-free" as well. Now faux fur is truly in the vernacular of fashion and luxury.

→ **The popularity of plant-based foods has soared in recent years. Have you noticed a change in the way people eat since you first opened Madame ZuZu's Emporium?**

Yes! People are far more open to trying new things, which is so wonderful. And the words "vegan" or "plant-based" are no longer taboo or associated with "no taste" like they used to be. Madame ZuZu's is a plant-based cafe that welcomes customers of all walks of life, whether it is their first time trying something plant-based or they're a lifelong vegan. Our mission is to serve great food for all to enjoy.

→ **You have friends coming to visit Highland Park for the first time. Apart from ZuZu's, where do you take them?**

Good question! We love Walker Bros. Pancake House, Del Rio, and Spirit Elephant!

MAISON ATIA
maisonatia.com

MADAME ZUZU'S EMPORIUM
1876 First Street
Highland Park, IL 60035

**WALKER BROS. PANCAKE HOUSE
(NOT VEGAN)**
620 Central Avenue
Highland Park, IL 60035

DEL RIO
228 Green Bay Road
Highwood, IL 60040

SPIRIT ELEPHANT
924 Green Bay Road
Winnetka, IL 60093

THE CHICAGO DINER

→ **2333 N MILWAUKEE AVENUE
CHICAGO, IL 60647**

→ **3411 N HALSTED STREET
CHICAGO, IL 60657**

1983 was a classic year. *Flashdance* came out, the internet was officially created, and I was born, an event that remarkably failed to make news headlines. It was also the year that The Chicago Diner debuted its meat-free menu.

This diner-in-the-rough goes against every expectation of what a vegan restaurant should look like. Founders Jo Kaucher and Mickey Hornick, a former commodities trader, made it their mission to re-create the quintessential American diner experience while bypassing the beef and the hippie palaver that was associated with vegetarian dining at the time.

There's some organic free-range eggs on the menu if you're so inclined, but for the most part, The Chicago Diner's dishes are vegan. Seitan features prominently as the protein de jour (in bacon, deli meat, chorizo, and chicken wing form) despite the influx of new meat alternatives that have flooded the market in recent years. I'm also triggered by the plant-based cheese options, which could definitely use an update (I'm biased, but I really do think concoctions based on coconut oil, starch, palm oil, and other additives have had their day). But the less contemporary ingredients are also part of what gives this restaurant its charm. I'm here for it, and like the locals, I'll keep coming back.

HANDLEBAR

VEGETARIAN | VEGAN OPTIONS AVAILABLE

→ **2311 W NORTH AVENUE
CHICAGO, IL 60647**

Handlebar is a small neighborhood eatery that serves *dinner* for breakfast Monday to Friday. That's a big draw for me; I've never understood why we limit ourselves to avocado toast and bird food in the morning when we could be eating a burger, lasagna, or a full plate of nachos and a michelada before heading to the office.

Handlebar is all about handmade comfort food—all vegan or vegetarian—served without pretense. It's a casual kind of venue where anything goes as long as you're not being a dickhead. On weekends, the breakfast menu draws a crowd; it's served until 3 p.m. and should tide you over until the dinner menu lights up. Vegan diners can sub out the organic eggs in any dish for tofu scramble, but my advice is to make a beeline for the chimichanga, burrito, chili mac attack, or vegan diablos (served with seitan chorizo, black beans, chipotle sauce, brown rice, and hand-pressed corn tostadas).

I'm not usually one for brand merch, but I will say the tees and prints that Handlebar sells are some of the best I've ever seen.

LIBERATION KITCHEN

VEGAN

→ **2054 W GRAND AVENUE
CHICAGO, IL 60612**

I remember the first time I noticed Liberation Kitchen's (formerly Upton's Naturals) products in the grocery store. I picked up a package of curious-looking "jackfruit meat," excited that vegan food branding was finally getting a makeover. I was also pleased to see a simple list of ingredients on the back.

It reminded me of something you don't often find in conventional supermarkets and convenience stores these days: actual food that, at some point, was grown in the ground.

Today, I'm still a fan of Upton's products, particularly the jackfruit and banana blossom meal bases. But what's particularly cool about this company is that their factory break room is open to the public, so you can try their full catalog of products, cooked by the pros themselves, seven days a week. The menu reminds me of a corner deli or college cafeteria, with a range of sandwiches, donuts, and the odd croissant or sausage roll—only in this case, it's all natural and animal-free.

KITCHEN 17

VEGAN

→ **2554 W DIVERSEY AVENUE
CHICAGO, IL 60647**

I think we've moved beyond the "Is vegan cheese allowed to be called cheese?" conversation. Seriously, it's only the pro-dairy lobbyists who are still keeping that debate alive (read the room, guys: nobody else cares). What we *should* be debating is what constitutes a real pizza.

Should it be a floppy, New York–style number, dripping with sauce and requiring a full fold-over to consume it? Or should it be a thick wedge of pie, with a deep-fried crust encapsulating innards of cheese and pepperoni? Should it even have cheese at all? (The answer to that is always yes; otherwise, we're talking about flatbread, not pizza.) Either way, Kitchen 17 will have your preference covered with fully veganized versions of the American pizza classics.

If your definition of pizza is a more minimally adorned, Italian, thin-crust affair, I can't help you. This is not the place. But I do recommend pivoting to one of Kitchen 17's burgers instead, which can be ordered with your choice of veggie, Impossible, or Beyond patties. The purists won't like this, but if you're feeling wild, go for the pizza burger.

Kitchen 17 also offers a suite of appetizers, like nachos, cauliflower wings, spinach dip, and salads for those looking to up their intake of greens.

LAND
LAND
LAND
LAND
LAND

CLEVELAND

According to history and Wikipedia, rock 'n' roll was invented in Cleveland. Wait, what?!

Turns out it's true. The style of music itself is rooted in African-American culture, like many of the genres we enjoy today. Back in the day ("the day" being sometime in the 1950s), rhythm and blues music was picking up mainstream popularity. Noticing the sudden traction, a Cleveland record store owner named Leo Mintz coined the term *rock 'n' roll* in a very unwoke move to distance the music from its black origins. He then teamed up with a local radio presenter named Alan Freed, who began playing rock songs on his late-night radio show. The genre took off from there.

The Moondog Coronation Ball, held in 1952 at the Cleveland Arena, is believed to be the first ever rock 'n' roll concert (at least the first to officially use the phrase). It was advertised as "the most terrible ball of them all!", and it gave serious Sex Pistols vibes but without the safety pins and bratty punk attitude.

If you're keen to learn more, swing by the **Rock & Roll Hall of Fame**, the official national museum dedicated to the genre. College students are eligible for discounted tickets, but Cleveland locals get in for free. Let me also take this opportunity to recognize some rock legends who happen to be vegan: Morrissey, Travis Barker (don't you dare @ me; he's still a musician!), Thom Yorke, Rob Zombie, and Sir Paul McCartney. You might find them acknowledged within the walls of the museum or on a visit to one of Cleveland's plant-based eateries next time they're on tour.

Now I'm not a sporty kinda girl and I never got into gaming, but I am highly competitive by nature. And for some reason, that ruthless streak has manifested in the art of pinball. I freakin' love pinnies (Aussie slang for "pinball"), as it was a weekend ritual of mine throughout childhood. My dad's training curriculum was structured and relentless, almost verging on *Dance Moms* territory, but by the age of ten, I had developed advanced gaming skills, excellent reflexes, and a number-one position on the leaderboard. Nobody my age appreciated this achievement, but it's a passion I've maintained into adulthood. So you can imagine my excitement when I came across Cleveland's **Superelectric Pinball Parlor**. Why it's not prominently featured on the local tourism board's website, I cannot say, but the venue is open to all ages, which means I can happily beat the asses of thirteen-year-olds on the *Goosebumps* machine. Entry is only $6 and gives you unlimited play. You can take your own food into the venue, so be sure to stock up on your favorite plant-based snacks ahead of time.

If you're one of those maniacal fitness types who prefers a different type of sport, I suggest taking your irritating energy levels to **Lake Erie**. It seems like a good place to annoy people with Crossfit routines. But for the more casual outdoors enthusiast, it's also a lovely place for bike riding, paddle boarding, hiking, or a plant-based picnic.

ROCK & ROLL HALL OF FAME
Union Home Mortgage Plaza
1100 Rock and Roll Boulevard
Cleveland, OH 44114

SUPERELECTRIC PINBALL PARLOR
6500 Detroit Avenue
Cleveland, OH 44102

LAKE ERIE
4101 Fulton Parkway
Cleveland, OH 44144

MUNCH

→ **28500 MILES ROAD, SUITE J
SOLON, OH 44139**

Fact: The food sold at grocery stores is generally never fresh, despite the claims of advertising. It's often shipped across long distances before it reaches the shelf, and is subject to fluctuating temperatures and lengthy periods in warehouse storage. To withstand that whole logistical journey, manufacturers must add preservatives and other additives to give the food the desired shelf life, which in some cases can be 12 months or more.

As Munch points out, mega-chain restaurants often do the same thing to achieve cost efficiencies. Coleslaw will arrive in enormous plastic drums, never going moldy; burger buns remain freakishly soft for weeks; cheese is pre-grated and coated with cellulose and starch to keep it from clumping together. Don't ask how long it's been sitting in the fridge; it's still good.

But that's not how Munch operates. This Mediterranean deli specializes in plant-based meals, and due to the restrictions of a tiny kitchen, there's no space to stockpile. Instead, fresh and local ingredients are sourced daily as needed. It's a refreshing change from the American food system's status quo.

Munch has been serving healthy breakfasts, soups, salads, sandwiches, and wraps for over 17 years now, all from their outpost at Case Western Reserve University. And despite its vintage aesthetic, the small eatery remains popular as ever with the student crowd.

You'll still find meat and dairy on the menu here, so don't assume that everything is plant-based. But it's all real food, and the path from producer to plate is short.

CLEVELAND VEGAN

VEGAN

→ **17112 DETROIT AVENUE**
LAKEWOOD, OH 44107

Cleveland Vegan founders Laura Ross and Justin Gorski never intended to have a restaurant. About 12 years ago, the pair went vegan while Ross worked as a yoga instructor and coordinator at a local women's shelter and Gorski worked at a catering company. Understandably, it quickly reached the point where Gorski struggled to work with meat products in his day job.

So at nights, the pair would play around in the kitchen, veganizing their favorite foods and tapping into Gorski's culinary creativity. That's how the idea for a vegan catering company got started.

As the company grew, the founders still missed the days of going out for a decent vegan breakfast—you know, a good breakfast sandwich, biscuits and gravy, or eggs. Local cafe options were sadly lackluster. That's when their catering business began to evolve into a brick-and-mortar brunch destination, then a lunch and dinner spot, until it eventually realized its final form as an all-day bakery and cafe.

The menu here is varied and accommodating, with clear options for those on nut-free, soy-free and gluten-free diets. Nothing's overly complicated, just simple and nourishing crowd pleasers, like avocado toast, loaded nachos, cheddar broccoli soup bowls, and comforting sandwiches. Pancakes and biscuits and gravy hang around long after the breakfast party's over, and are available on the menu until 9 p.m. If you're a fan of superfood smoothies and fancy lattes, Cleveland Vegan is your fam. They offer matcha, maca, turmeric, pea protein, and primo alternative milks as well as a Bulletproof blend.

Through a partnership with Oberlin Food Hub, the business is able to source its ingredients locally and organically from a collective of small farms. I like this model because it allows small independent producers to connect with businesses they might not normally have access to and overcome some of the challenges associated with distribution in our food supply chain.

There's multiple facets to this enterprise. The adjoining bakery offers takeaway cupcakes, cookies, donuts, pies, pastries, and cakes baked to order. Meanwhile, the original catering arm continues to feed everyone, from small groups to Kardashian-scale wedding parties.

5 MINUTES WITH

LAURA ROSS

CLEVELAND VEGAN

Laura hasn't always worked in the food industry; her background is in social work. While the two career paths may appear unrelated, her experience working with—and deeply understanding—the human condition has prepared her well for the challenges of managing a cafe team.

"I've always wanted to have some meaning behind what I'm doing. I started doing social work in my mid-twenties. I always felt compelled to strengthen the voice of other women, which is what I did at a women's shelter. I felt very called to that. When we started Cleveland Vegan, I was pregnant, and I gave birth while the business was exploding. I found myself with an infant and a full-time job at a domestic violence center, then I'd come home and work on a very demanding business. When I knew the business needed me, I realized I'd have to leave the center.

"I've always had the mentality of wanting to give back, and I didn't feel like I was giving that up by leaving. I felt like I was now feeding people in a way that was not harmful to the environment, animals, or their bodies, which felt great.

"Before this, I was a volunteer coordinator at a women's shelter, where I conducted a 40-hour crisis intervention training for volunteers and interns. They'd work on the hotline and as justice system advocates in the courts.

"That experience has definitely proved helpful for what I do today. See, if you're in the restaurant industry, you're working with people who are predominantly under 25, and they're going through life stuff, all the dramas you were going through at that age. A few years ago, I found myself missing social work, but it's occurred to me more recently that I'm still doing that kind of work, just in a different capacity."

CLEVELAND VEGAN'S ALMOND RICOTTA

2 cups whole skinless almonds
(soaked in cold water)

1¼ cups water

½ tbsp salt

¼ tsp black pepper

1½ tbsp finely minced red onion

2 cloves finely minced garlic

1 tbsp nutritional yeast

1 tbsp lemon juice

½ tbsp agave

1 tbsp chopped parsley

Place soaked almonds and water in a blender, then blend until completely smooth. It may take 5 to 10 minutes to become completely smooth. In a bowl, add all remaining ingredients. Fold in blended almonds until all ingredients are thoroughly combined. Refrigerate. This lasts up to a week in the fridge.

Add to pasta dishes to give them a rich creaminess. Put it inside a savory crepe along with your favorite veggies. Spread on toast for breakfast (if you're tired of boring avocado toast). We love to add almond ricotta to anything we can. It is so delicious and creamy.

NOTES

Almonds need to soak for at least two hours before blending. If you're in a rush, soak them in hot water for faster results.

If you are unable to find skinless almonds, skin-on almonds will work as well. You just won't get that nice white look that classic ricotta has.

A high-powered blender, like a Vitamix, will give you the best results.

ALADDIN'S EATERY

VEGAN OPTIONS AVAILABLE

→ **CHECK THEIR WEBSITE (ALADDINS.COM) FOR A LOCATION NEAR YOU.**

The Aladdin's story begins with Lebanese immigrant Fady Chamoun, who arrived in the United States in 1972 brimming with entrepreneurial spirit and a vision to bring healthy Lebanese cuisine to an American audience. It was a slow burn for Fady, but he achieved his dream; in 1994, he opened the first Aladdin's Eatery venue alongside his wife Sally and, over time, grew the business into a restaurant chain with over 30 locations spanning four states. Now, Fady is an award-winning entrepreneur, philanthropist, activist, and CEO of the Seasoned Brands restaurant group. And it all started with hummus.

Lebanese food, by nature, is very vegan-friendly. Take away the obvious grilled meats and kofta, and much of it is vegan or vegetarian, focusing on ancient grains, vegetables, nuts, and pulses.

While there's a handful of dishes at Aladdin's that involve chicken, beef, or lamb, the menu is dominated by animal-free options. There's salads, pita wraps, and, my favorite, the pitza (a pita bread pizza) as well as soups, fresh smoothies, and of course, hummus.

The Mediterranean diet has long been recognized as one of the healthiest in the world and far removed from some of the overprocessed junk that represents modern society's convenience culture. So regardless of dietary preference, you can't go wrong with natural, freshly prepared food, which is precisely what you'll find at Aladdin's.

THE VEGAN DOUGHNUT COMPANY

VEGAN

→ **14811 DETROIT AVENUE
LAKEWOOD, OH 44107**

You don't hear many people refer to themselves as vegetarian these days. At some point over the past couple of decades, it seems a memo went out to all vegetarians that was like, "Hey, you're already halfway there. Why not go full vegan and stop half-assing it." My notification clearly went to the spam folder, but it's the best explanation I can think of to explain the mass cultural shift.

The Vegan Doughnut Company begins with a similar story of transition. Sisters Kharisma and Kyra Mayo spent a large chunk of their lives as committed vegetarians before embracing a fully vegan diet in 2014. Problem was, the lifestyle ruled out one of their favorite foods: donuts. There simply weren't any vegan alternatives available on the streets of Ohio.

So the sisters got to work and created their own solution, experimenting in their home kitchen before refining their process and recipes and taking them public with the opening of The Vegan Doughnut Company. Nowadays, you can purchase their handmade creations at their Lakewood store, but be aware that it's often busy and pre-orders cannot be taken, so you need to get in fast to score a bundle of treats.

The year-round menu includes traditional flavors, like old fashioned (with vanilla glaze) and chocolate sprinkles, but the monthly rotation is where things get exciting. Recent highlights include passionfruit and sprinkles, choco taco cake, raspberry strudel, as well as a celebratory "Pride Heart" (I didn't try this, but I'm hoping it's rainbow-colored and maybe a bit sparkly).

While there aren't any gluten-free options on the menu, the donuts are 100% animal-free, and no nuts are used in their making.

5 MINUTES WITH

KIRSTEN SUTARIA

COFOUNDER AT DOOZY POTS

Kirsten is the cofounder and "Chief of Curious Creation" at Wonderlab's Doozy Pots, an organic plant-based gelato company, which she founded with her husband Karl in 2019.

→ **Tell us a little bit about Doozy Pots and what inspired you to create a plant-based brand.**

My background is in food science and product development, and I have worked with ice cream for 13 years. I spend a lot of my time doing ingredient and product research, and back in 2018, I became really interested in the potential of hemp as a food. It is a sustainable crop, and it's loaded with healthy fats and proteins; to me, it was a no-brainer to use it as an earth-friendly dairy alternative, but due to the prohibition of hemp in the US until 2019, there was very little innovation with it.

I spent a year working on ingredient sourcing and recipe development, and we then moved from London to Cleveland to start Doozy Pots. We are still just a small, two-person team, but we have gained national distribution with Sprouts, taking us to 25 states in total.

→ **You have friends coming to visit Cleveland. Where do you take them to eat?**

For a "meat and potatoes" town, Cleveland has a really fantastic plant-based scene! For lunch, I'm hitting **Cleveland Vegan, Zaytoon Lebanese Kitchen, Beet Jar**, or **Tommy's**. In the evening, it would be **Cloak and Dagger** or **Forage Public House** for their chicken and waffles made with oyster mushrooms. If you're in the mood for sushi, **Blue Sushi Sake Grill** and **Sakana** have extensive menus of veggie sushi too.

→ **Do you have any local shopping tips for home cooks or Cleveland gems you're willing to share?**

The **North Union Farmers' Market** is a great place to find local produce and plant-based products. **Heinen's** grocery stores are a local Cleveland gem, and they do a fantastic job of bringing in local products and produce. **Beet Jar**, **The Grocery Kitchen and Market**, and **Birch Cafe** are all well-curated markets with vegan goodies and prepared foods.

I'm from New York, so this is a little crazy to say, but Cleveland is home to some of the best bagels of all time. **Cleveland Bagel** is an absolute gem, and my go-to is a rosemary and sea salt bagel with house-made vegan "schmear," lettuce, tomato, avocado, and onion.

Speaking of sandwiches, **Ritual Juicery** makes an awesome sandwich called "The Sammy," with house-made carrot lox, cucumber, avocado, radish, romaine, and onions.

Definitely do a trip to Waterloo Arts District for a "Sammy" and to check out the **Pop Life** building, which features a mural by Camille Walala.

My go-to coffee shop is **Phoenix**. They make oat milk in-house, and there's no upcharge!

CLEVELAND VEGAN
See p. 47

ZAYTOON LEBANESE KITCHEN
1150 Huron Road East
Cleveland, OH 44115

TOMMY'S
1824 Coventry Road
Cleveland Heights, OH 44118

CLOAK AND DAGGER
2399 W 11th Street
Cleveland, OH 44113

FORAGE PUBLIC HOUSE
14600 Detroit Avenue
Lakewood, OH 44107

BLUE SUSHI SAKE GRILL
2000 Crocker Road
Westlake, OH 44145

SAKANA
19300 Detroit Road
Rocky River, OH 44116

NORTH UNION FARMERS' MARKET

HEINEN'S DOWNTOWN
900 Euclid Avenue
Cleveland, OH 44115

BEET JAR
1432 W 29th Street
Cleveland, OH 44113

THE GROCERY KITCHEN AND MARKET
2600 Detroit Avenue
Cleveland, OH 44113

BIRCH CAFÉ
5557 Wilson Mills Road
Highland Heights, OH 44143

THE CLEVELAND BAGEL COMPANY
4201 Detroit Avenue
Cleveland, OH 44113

MBUS
MBUS
MBUS
MBUS
MBUS

I've never heard of a college grad who snatched up their degree, packed their bags, and set out to chase their dreams in ... Columbus. But let's not discount its potential just yet; the city is known for its low cost of living, prosperous economy, and plentiful job opportunities. With that in mind, it's no surprise that Columbus appeals to millennials who'd prefer some breathing space in the Midwest as opposed to, say, bunking in a 250-square-foot Brooklyn studio apartment above a dry cleaner.

According to Census data, the average age of Columbus residents is only 32 years old. That core demographic is clearly reflected by the city's food scene, which is vibrant, diverse, and built on a community of small, independent vendors, from farm-to-table restaurants to small-batch breweries and coffee shops.

Sadly, many of these businesses closed during the pandemic. Thin operating margins combined with stay-at-home orders made it impossible for small operators to stay afloat. On the upside, given the city's recent history of growth, the hospitality industry seems to be bouncing back quickly, unveiling a new generation of restaurants with it. Here are a few that are worth checking out next time you're in town.

COLUMBUS

WOODHOUSE VEGAN

VEGAN | WOMAN-OWNED

→ **851 N FOURTH STREET
COLUMBUS, OH 43215**

Best known for its vegan comfort food, this lady-led family business is about as close as you can get to a home-cooked meal without flying home to visit your mom. The menu gets my stomach tingling within the first few lines: there's award-winning mac and cheese that's fully veganized, allergen-friendly, and served as a whopping dollop of cheddar-y noodles; fish tacos, reminiscent of a McDonald's fish sandwich; and delicious bowls of nachos with chips stacked on their sides in an act of structural ingenuity that ensures each mouthful receives an equal dose of flavor.

Everything is made in-house, primarily from seasonal ingredients, but that's not the point. The goal here is to re-create those classic dishes and food memories we enjoyed as kids (and keep returning to as adults) while keeping animals out of the equation.

In addition to restaurant meals and takeout, guests can preorder from a generous selection of Woodhouse Vegan bakery items, including sweet pies, pastries, cookies, and cakes. I usually pretend I'm having a party of some kind so my large order doesn't seem so conspicuous, when in reality it's just me having a really good night in with an eight-inch birthday cake.

SEITAN'S REALM

VEGAN

→ **3496 N HIGH STREET**
COLUMBUS, OH 43214

One doesn't need to be vegan to enjoy animal-free protein. Seitan's Realm proves that point clearly through the vessel of enormous sandwiches that are packed with deli meat, oozing with sauces, and delivering big hits of mouth-watering umami.

Imagine a toasted onion roll crammed with thinly sliced mounds of seitan roast beef and cheese sauce. Add seasoned curly fries and onion rings, and you've got a vegan version of Arby's. According to the Seitan's Realm team, this "Beeef N Chedduh" re-creation is probably the most popular item on the menu, spanning back to the days when Seitan's Realm was just a small food truck. But now that they've found a permanent brick-and-mortar location on High Street, the team can sling sandwiches all day long without fear of inciting a riot due to product shortages.

Don't limit yourself to the classics, though. If something's out of stock, try something new. That could mean poppers, mac and cheese, wings, gyros, Reubens, or the Anarchy Burger (an onion bun containing two seitan burger patties topped with vegan cheddar cheese, onion, pickles, Thousand Island dressing, and lettuce). Early birds can also pick at a concise breakfast menu that features a couple of sandwiches, waffles, biscuits, and gravy.

Do people ever confuse this vegan deli for a satanic house of worship? Founder Kevin Ridenbaugh explains:

"I was talking to my friend one day about dumb ideas for names, and he said 'Dude, you make everything with seitan. You should put that in the name. Give it something edgy; don't be the Happy Little Hut or something.'

"We thought the name was funny and used these two goats on our logo to make it look satanic, just kind of push the edge a little. I think people are drawn to it; it's just fun. Some people say they'll never come here because of the name and imagery, but whatever.

"There's nothing in the logo that's actually satanic. We also love horror movies, so the inside of the deli is dedicated to monster movies. We have *Friday the 13th* posters, a Freddie Kruger claw, and a Michael Meyers mask..."

I'm there.

5 MINUTES WITH

CARA WOODHOUSE

CO-OWNER, WOODHOUSE VEGAN

→ **First up, tell me about the restaurant.**

The idea behind the restaurant is to do comfort food. We don't hold back on taste, texture, salt, fat, or sugar. It's all the stuff you don't think you'd be able to eat as a vegan. But we wanted to be an inclusive space, a place where people could bring their entire family and not leave thinking, "I'm so hungry; all I ate was grass."

So we wanted to do our spin on the food we grew up eating, things like Steak and Shake, McDonald's, loaded nachos, fish tacos, pasta, mac and cheese. People referred to it as "stoner casual" when we first opened, and I thought, "Alright ... I guess that hits the nail on the head."

→ **What's it like running a vegan business in Columbus as opposed to somewhere like NYC or LA?**

LA is so saturated and expensive, but it's becoming expensive here in Columbus too, especially for the area that we're in downtown. We're adjacent to the Short North Arts district, which used to be gritty, but now it's starting to be bought out by big box retailers. We're around the corner, a little bit off the beaten path in the Italian Village, where it's still got a grittiness to it that we like.

We love the area. My sisters and I have lived, worked, and played here for over two decades now, so it made sense to open our restaurant in this neighborhood.

Columbus is somewhat of a hub for starter restaurants, a great test market. In fact, White Castle and Wendy's were started right here in Columbus. It's also an awesome cultural hub, with a lot of diversity within a small area. It really gives you the opportunity to explore.

→ Any local tips for those visiting Columbus for the first time?

Our favorite pizza is **Paulie Gee's**, which originated in Brooklyn. They make a cashew ricotta, a vegan sausage, and the vegan pizza menu is just as extensive as the traditional one. A good portion of sales are vegan, and a lot of staff are as well.

Comune popped up around the same time as us, but it's more of a fine-dining concept. So we go there for celebrations. They're not completely vegan—you can add cheese or egg—but they're plant-forward and do amazing vegan substitutions.

Other recommendations would be **Northstar Cafe** and **Brassica**. At this point in Columbus, you're hard-pressed to walk into a restaurant and not find at least one vegan or vegetarian item on the menu. It feels progressive, especially compared to some other cities.

PAULIE GEE'S
1195 N High Street
Columbus, OH 43201

COMUNE
677 Parsons Avenue
Columbus, OH 43206

NORTHSTAR CAFE
For locations,
thenorthstarcafe.com/locations

BRASSICA
For locations, brassicas.com/
locations

PORTIA'S CAFE

VEGAN

→ **4428 INDIANOLA AVENUE**
   COLUMBUS, OH 43214

Dedicated vegan eateries are relatively hard to come by in Columbus, so if you're committed to the cause, make Portia's the first pit stop on your eating tour. And with a menu that's 100% vegan, non-GMO, and gluten-free, expect to be returning often.

Meal options here are expansive, with a heavy lean on fresh vegetables and pulses. Aside from the large range of soups, salads, and breakfast dishes, there's pizzadillas, quesadillas, and wraps, which seem to be Portia's specialty. Order them any way you'd like, whether it be stuffed with leafy green superfoods, tofu, falafel, or a made-from-scratch, raw-nut-based patty. If you're a low-carber, ask for a bowl or lettuce wrap. They're all about flexible options here.

Now, I don't get why people are so obsessed with hummus in the United States. I agree that it's very tasty, but I feel we're missing out on so much more. That's why I was excited to discover a whole range of non-hummus-based dips available at Portia's, including spinach-artichoke, salsa, guacamole, and "notuna" (made from walnuts). I respect you, hummus ... but you've served your time. It's time to step aside.

Dietary inclusivity is an overarching theme throughout Portia's menu, which provides much-appreciated assurance for those with allergies and food intolerances. All ingredients are gluten-free by default, and the team is committed to sourcing organic, local produce wherever possible. My only gripe is that their plant-based cheese offering could use an upgrade (sorry, Daiya, I'm just saying what we're all thinking). Reach out to me, Portia's. Let's talk hemp cheese.

PATTYCAKE BAKERY

VEGAN

→ **3870 N HIGH STREET COLUMBUS, OH 43214**

Ever heard of a Worker-Owned Cooperative (WOC)? It's a business structure in which no CEO or corporate hierarchy exists, and employees are treated as co-owners, participating in all aspects of operating the business and its finances. Not only does this create meaningful jobs within a community, it means that employees are invested in the success of the business and are not just there to clock in and out for the benefit of someone else's pocket.

Pattycake Bakery is one such WOC, and it's currently managed by eight co-owners, including its founder, who originally opened the store in 2003. Aside from supporting sustainable employment models and eco-friendly initiatives (such as a local bicycle delivery service), their mission is to create handmade vegan baked goods from natural ingredients. For the most part, that takes the form of cakes, cookies, muffins, and the occasional granola.

A selection of cakes are available daily (Wednesday to Sunday) to pick up in-store or custom order. In particular, look out for the zodiac series of cakes (correct: they are inspired by star signs), which are phenomenal. If you visit during Gemini season, expect a purple and white coconut concoction with raspberry and chocolate ganache.

If you're in the mood for entertaining, I strongly suggest ordering a "take and bake" tray, which will warm your kitchen with the aroma of freshly baked treats and trick your houseguests into thinking you're actually a skilled cook.

DAL
DAL
DAL
DAL
DAL

I've never had a frozen margarita before—I'm more of a rum or whiskey kind of girl—but Dallas claims to be the official home of this popular beverage. A local restaurateur invented the frozen margarita machine here about 50 years ago, and the city is now committed to owning that title. It even sports a Margarita Mile, a self-guided tour of bars and restaurants that each serve their own spin on the classic. But I'm going to level with you: outside of the alcoholic beverages, it's not easy to find plant-based options in Dallas.

Honkin' slabs of smoky barbeque? Yes. Corn dogs and lobster rolls dripping in warm butter? Plenty to be found. But chickpea burgers? Not a strong suit for this city. Don't worry, though, as I've plucked out a few gems for you.

Where Dallas does come through is on the sustainable travel front. In 2016, Dallas/Fort Worth International Airport became the first carbon-neutral airport in the world. It was a multipronged strategy, involving electric and hybrid vehicles, increased investment in public transport, and the implementation of technology to decrease heat and lighting usage. But it clearly wasn't enough for the airport's management team because now it's striving for a new environmental goal: net zero carbon emissions by 2030, which would set a new benchmark for sustainable travel in the United States.

When I travel, I usually stay at Airbnbs instead of hotels since I like to bring my tiny and extremely high-maintenance toy poodle with me everywhere I go (this way I can search for places that have a nice patch of grass for him to run around). But if you've got the budget to blow on a hotel, take a look at Dallas's Kimpton Pittman in Deep Ellum. The hotel restaurant, **Elm & Good**, is a distinct step above the standard chain hotel brasserie and serves genuinely interesting vegetarian and gluten-free options, such as Lion's Mane mushroom cake and a hearty paella made with mushroom stalk "chorizo."

ELM & GOOD
2551 Elm Street
Dallas, TX 75226

SPIRAL DINER & BAKERY

VEGAN | WOMAN-OWNED

→ **1314 W MAGNOLIA AVENUE**
FORT WORTH, TX 76104

The Spiral series of eateries emerged in 2002, when founder Amy McNutt realized she was sent to this earth with a purpose: to make vegan food so tasty, nobody would have an excuse not to try it.

And that's really all Spiral Diner asks: just try it. No preaching, no tree-hugging, no hippie hyperbole. Just try a little cashew-quinoa patty or a bite of a vegan Reuben sandwich. Go on, have a nudge. Slather it in vegan Swiss cheese sauce and mustard, and let it dribble seductively through your fingers. Succumb to the flavor, and don't overthink it.

Locals come here for diner food that's mindfully made (as opposed to the culinary disaster roadside diners are typically famous for). But just because it's vegan doesn't mean it's afraid of getting dirty. The sandwiches come bursting at the crust-seams with potato chips on the side (try the baked potato grilled cheese, which includes fries, vegan bacon bits, sour cream, green onion, melted cheese, and a bit of ranch for dipping), and the Triple Double burger, which subs grilled cheese sandwiches in place of burger buns, is enough to feed a family of four. Or just me after a 45-minute Peloton class. At least that's how I interpret Spiral's mission statement.

BELSE PLANT CUISINE

VEGAN

→ **1910 PACIFIC AVENUE, SUITE 1400 (FIRST FLOOR)
DALLAS, TX 75201**

There's a popular plant-based restaurant in LA called Little Pine, located in the meandering hipster neighborhood of Silverlake. It's known more for the fact that Moby once owned it than it is for food, even though the dance music mogul is no longer in the picture. However, Little Pine's current owners have built on that original restaurant concept with the creation of Dallas's very own Belse Plant Cuisine.

There's some crossover between the two restaurant menus, such as fancy fries, fennel flatbread, and watermelon sushi—all of which appear at both locations. For Belse (and Little Pine for that matter), the idea is to re-create a traditional restaurant menu, albeit without animal ingredients. It's a little upmarket and a little casual, with a broad menu that includes burgers, pastas, soups, empanadas, and a small range of desserts.

Pay close attention to the Belse logo; it was created by street art legend Shepard Fairey, the man behind the global OBEY motif that's been plastered on everything from brick walls to $200 T-shirts.

SPIRAL DINER & BAKERY (*see* p. 70)

BELSE PLANT CUISINE (*see* p. 71)

KALACHANDJI'S (*see* p. 74)

KALACHANDJI'S

VEGETARIAN | VEGAN OPTIONS AVAILABLE

→ **5430 GURLEY AVENUE**
   DALLAS, TX 75223

Kalachandji's arrived on the (relatively unknown) vegetarian scene almost four decades ago, back when "plant-based" dining wasn't even a phrase yet. It's genuinely impressive that in a place like Dallas—which is typically known for its bountiful hunks of barbecued brisket—this vegetarian restaurant has stood its ground for so long. But with our newfound collective focus on health and wellness, Kalachandji's has finally found itself, deservingly, in the spotlight.

The focus here is on Ayurvedic cooking, a style of "conscious" cuisine that explores how different ingredients react together and affect the body when combined. Exactly how specific foods affect the body will change from person to person (or even from day to day), but the guiding principle is designed to minimize digestive issues and help folks eat what makes them feel good and thrive.

While the menu is predominantly lacto-vegetarian, vegan diners are welcomingly accommodated. By nature of the cuisine, meat, fish, eggs, onion, and garlic are all absent from the menu. I'll admit that I was all in until the onion and garlic bit, but perhaps I need to get out of my comfort zone. And who knows, maybe eliminating those ingredients from my diet will alleviate all the bloating I get when I eat (because it's definitely got nothing to do with the fact that I ate a whole pizza in minutes).

The food is served buffet-style, but think of it more like a classy buffet—none of that trashy cafeteria business. I'm not sure exactly how to explain the decor here, but it's a vibe, certainly more extravagant than I was expecting. Like ... it's a lot.

The menu changes daily, but the options are always plentiful and fresh. You can expect a range of curries, mixed vegetables, rice, and lentil dishes complemented with pickles, chutneys, and homemade breads. There's always a dessert or two available, and if you're already familiar with Indian sweets, you'll have a great time (I'm already dreaming of the mango cashew halva).

The Kalachandji's team operates a vegetarian cooking school on site, and in my opinion, the $35 classes are a fantastic deal, considering they also include dinner. But if you want to leave the cooking to the experts, come for the Tai Chi, meditation, and Ayurveda classes instead.

RECIPE OAK CLIFF

VEGAN

→ **1831 S EWING AVENUE
DALLAS, TX 75216**

If you've got the disposable income and mobility to enjoy a vegan foodie adventure, chances are you don't live in a food desert. That's an area where high-quality, nutritious food is not readily available or affordable, a place where grocery stores offer limited options (if there's one nearby), and organic farmers' markets are nowhere in sight. So, not Beverly Hills.

But in the pocket of Dallas where Recipe Oak Cliff is located, food security is a big problem, and this standalone takeout spot is considered a diamond in the rough.

Operated through the Susu Cultural Business Incubator, Recipe Oak Cliff provides a hub for small food businesses to share kitchen space and connect with the community. Their menu focuses on nutritious vegan and soy-free meals, and while choices are limited, the food is tasty, affordable, and fresh.

A selection of seasonal raw juices and smoothies is available. They also serve tacos, which come in three styles: barbeque jackfruit, chipotle walnut, or pumpkin seed falafel and hummus, with either soft tortilla shells or lettuce cups. There are also a few hearty salads and a true veggie burger, which is made from oats, vegetables, and herbs (not a fleck of soy protein to be found).

It's not Starbucks, so don't expect to settle into a table for the afternoon with your laptop and start streaming *Stranger Things*. But you can call to order ahead, and there's plenty of parking available for a quick pickup.

Plush with greenery in the summer, serene ski slopes in the winter, and nestled at the base of the Rocky Mountains, Denver is the antithesis of New York's bustling grayscale metropolis. Its picturesque urban landscape makes it a popular destination for outdoorsy folk who seek their thrills hiking, biking, and camping. Basically all of the activities I don't like because they involve natural elements that mess up my hair.

Situated 5820 feet above sea level (which gives Denver the name "Mile High City"—just in case you thought the nickname referred to something else), it may take time for your body to adjust to the altitude and air quality. For that reason, first-time visitors should take time to relax and acclimatize before hitting the nature trails. Maybe start with some snacks instead or, even better, a brew. There are around 100 local tap houses and brewing companies located within city limits, so allocate your designated driver now or book a hosted tour. That's the kind of trail I can get behind.

I highly recommend a stop at **Denver Beer Co.** because their facility is 100% fueled by solar power. Their forward-thinking sustainability plan also involves carbon dioxide capture technology, allowing the brewery to capture over 100,000 pounds of CO_2 per year, which can then be reused by other industries rather than emitted into the environment. If you need further reason to feel good about indulging in some brewskies, you can join their regular run club. Again, a fitness regime that speaks my language. I like how Denver operates.

For those with kids to entertain, skip the zoo (the captivity of animals has no place in this book) and head to an animal sanctuary instead. **Luvin Arms** is located a short drive from Denver in Erie, Colorado, and is home to a menagerie of rescued farm animals, including pigs, goats, horses, and lil' duckies.

DENVER

DENVER BEER CO.
denverbeerco.com

LUVIN ARMS
3470 County Road 7
Erie, CO 80516

SOMEBODY PEOPLE

VEGAN

→ **1165 S BROADWAY #104
DENVER, CO 80210**

Any restaurant that takes its name from a David Bowie song is a winner in my book. And it just so happens that this is my book.

Somebody People had already won me over with their venue decor alone. The space is dotted with the kind of quirky art that's reminiscent of the laneway coffee shops and pop-up galleries in Melbourne. The colorful, sunny interior invokes Sydney-side beach culture and acts as a stark contrast to the brick-blocked Denver city streets outside. All of this made complete sense when I discovered that the owners, Tricia and Sam Maher, are Aussies like me. This fact seems culturally significant because it guarantees that they'll make excellent coffee.

On the drinks menu, there's a short list of zero-proof cocktails featuring Seedlip, a non-alcoholic distilled spirit made from potent botanicals. It's delicate and sophisticated, but to kick off, I'm diving directly into the boozy Gap Year, a party blend of Jamaican rum, peach, pineapple, coconut, and lime.

Now for food, their menu is relatively short, featuring 13 sharing-style dishes that are simple (hummus spiked with a little sumac and chili oil) yet a little bit fancy (farinata with romano beans, skordalia, and scallions). There's always a couple of handmade pastas available, but luckily, dishes generally vary with the season.

During COVID, Somebody People partnered with different farms and suppliers and began offering a weekly fresh produce box that changed according to season. At a time when we were all missing in-person dining, it was an awesome way to grab some biodynamic wine and house-made pasta and re-create the restaurant experience at home. While it's no longer available, it was an indication that this is a business that has grit and is here to stay.

SO RADISH

VEGAN

→ **5711 OLDE WADSWORTH BOULEVARD
ARVADA, CO 80002**

When So Radish first opened in 2019, the intention was to lead with plant-based dishes while still serving meat as an optional side. The rationale made sense at first: create a space that vegan diners can enjoy while still appealing to their nonvegan mates, a place where eaters of all persuasions could coexist in the harmony of tacos and tinned beer without dissolving the fabric of their friendship due to irreconcilable political debate (i.e., where to go for lunch).

But ... the world has changed quite a bit since then. Trump was fired, and vegan eaters can now speak more freely without fear of persecution because companies like Tyson and Unilever decided that plant-based food was on trend. So, at this stage, I think it's safe to say that people no longer need meat at every meal to feel comfortable. The majority of folks probably wouldn't even notice if you swapped their beef patty for a Beyond one.

As far as decor goes, the realm of So Radish is a convergence of restaurant and discotheque, complete with neon lights, checkerboard floors, and a life-sized Elvis cutout at the door. Its late '80s/early '90s party time appeal doesn't just shine, though; it explodes with bright, wildly colorful wall murals, exposed ceilings, Vaporwave aesthetic, and an abundant use of the word "rad."

At the bar, stools stand like a rainbow of glossy bottle caps, while the spirits sit inside shelves shaped into oversized shutter-lens glasses. Here, you'll face your first key decision point: what to drink. There's a strong craft brew lineup (including a few gluten-free options), a catalog of ciders and vegan wine if you're going full throttle, or kombucha if you have work to do later in the day.

These days, the food menu leans heavily into fast casual, with fried cauliflower tacos, tempeh ribs, avocado fries, and more. There are a few salad options too, but let's be real: that's not what you came for.

Oh, and the meat options that were previously available? They're gone now. Didn't need them. Nobody's crying about it.

META BURGER

VEGAN

→ **7950 E MISSISSIPPI AVENUE DENVER, CO 80247**

→ **5505 W 20TH AVENUE EDGEWATER, CO 80214**

I received a message once from a customer who wanted to know if our Grounded hemp cheeses were fat-free. I said they were not because that would make a pretty terrible-tasting cheese, so they went full Karen and took to social media demanding that we "DO BETTER." If you're that person and you like to diet-shame those who want a little treat, keep walking because Meta Burger isn't here for you.

Meta Burger's concept is simple: unashamedly American fast food, but make it plant-based. Their deluxe chicken sandwich (with crispy fried vegan chicken, pickles, lettuce, tomato, and special sauce) feels far naughtier than it is, while the classic burger, which swaps beef for a soy patty, is equally convincing.

I'm unsure how I feel about the Flatiron, which features grilled mushrooms and shaved Brussels sprouts. I don't think it's going to win over your typical college frat boy after a night of beer pong, but I can't deny that it sounds delicious. I'm going to have to try it next time.

The staff won't lecture you about the fact that their burgers are more sustainable than the mass-produced meat variety, nor will they flex on the nutritional advantages. They could, but they choose not to. Because if we're really going to get nonvegans on board with protein alternatives, it's got to be about taste and convenience ... and that's where Meta Burger delivers.

BROTHERS BBQ

VEGAN OPTIONS AVAILABLE

→ **FOR ALL COLORADO LOCATIONS,**
VISIT BROTHERS-BBQ.COM.

You're just going to have to trust me on this one. YES, the value proposition of Brothers BBQ is to sell slow-cooked meat by the pound. So it's unlikely that any ethical vegan would venture close to such a place unless it was to conduct a protest. But if you're the flexitarian type and find yourself in the vicinity of a Brothers BBQ, I got you.

In a surprising twist, Brothers has given their vegan offering just as much menu space as the pork spare ribs and brisket. The BBQ tofu comes slathered in sweet sauce and is lightly charred on the grill, giving it that lovely caramelized, smoky flavor. They've also got the standard Impossible burger and a few vegetarian salad iterations you can order with tofu and without the dairy cheese.

Like many restaurants that now offer plant proteins, it's possible they'll use the same cooking equipment that's used for meat— understandable if that's a dealbreaker for you. For those who are still easing into the plant-based journey, having accessible options like this is critical. And think of the net impact: every time an omnivore chooses the meat-free option, it's one less sale going toward the support of animal agriculture.

SPUTNIK

VEGETARIAN | VEGAN OPTIONS AVAILABLE

→ **3 S BROADWAY**
DENVER, CO 80209

So you find yourself at Sputnik after a pleasant evening of live music at the Hi-Dive next door. Now it's after midnight, and as the bodies and lights surrounding you begin to blur, you're thinking it's a great idea to take off your shoes and dance. I'm going to guess that's got something to do with the four jalapeño-infused tequila shots from earlier. Nevertheless, in situations like this, emergency bar food is required, something to sponge up the alcoholic spirits. Most of the time, bars aren't in the business of vegan catering, so you might be tempted to make a radical compromise. But you're in luck because plant-based bar food is exactly what the good people at Sputnik do.

Almost all of the menu items are vegetarian or vegan here. While the venue isn't built for romantic anniversary dinners, you'll be set for snacks. Fries, field roast corn dogs, and cauliflower wings and tacos are go-to picks, followed by a selection of sandwiches starring jackfruit or falafel. Select a couple of small plates, remember to hydrate, and you should be in good stead come morning. If it's a weekend, you could even come back for brunch, which runs until 3 p.m., and get a decent tofu scramble or quinoa cake.

One of the smartest social-distancing tactics I've seen, the owners of Sputnik constructed life-sized "ghosts" made from wire, sheets, and various scraps to occupy certain booths and bar seats, ensuring that patrons won't sit too close together. I kinda hope they're still there the next time I visit because they were eerily comforting.

CITY, 'O CITY

**VEGETARIAN | VEGAN OPTIONS AVAILABLE |
WOMAN-OWNED**

→ **206 E 13TH AVENUE
DENVER, CO 80203**

Relaxed, welcoming, and unpretentious: those are the first words that come to mind when describing City, 'O City, one of Denver's best-known vegetarian restaurants. The menu operates from 10 a.m. until 11 p.m. each day, and drinks are poured throughout—from coffee in the morning to cocktails in the evening. Or if you work from home like me and no longer have any concept of time or space, cocktails in the morning.

Menu-wise, we've got a lot to work with. There's a lemon tarragon pasta finished with shaved vegan parmesan that's made by sister restaurant Watercourse Foods, udon noodles and chipotle bowls, chicken and waffles shaped out of hunks of fried cauliflower, seitan wings, salads, and plenty of sides. But I'm doubling down on the pizza, which is 25% off every Wednesday and can be made vegan by subbing the dairy with Daiya or cashew cheese. I strongly recommend the cashew version if you're faced with that choice.

There's more going on here than initially meets the eye. Gallery shows are held each month, with upcoming artists featured on the venue's walls and website, and the team operates a micro farm behind the scenes, giving their kitchen access to hyper-fresh produce in the warmer months. I also appreciate their transparency around staff pay and the distribution of tips, which is an issue that's become increasingly problematic in the hospitality industry in recent years (you can learn more about how City, 'O City is committed to fair pay on their website).

If your mind is still on the cocktails, I'd suggest heading over between 3 p.m. and 6 p.m. or 11 p.m. and 1 a.m., when happy hour is in full swing.

5 MINUTES WITH

ERIK AMUNDSON

COFOUNDER & CEO OF VEVOLUTION

Erik was one of the first people I met in the plant-based community when I moved to the States. We've stayed in touch ever since, and these days he's the head honcho at Vevolution, a global vegan business and investment marketplace. He started working with plant-based brands in 2019 and has spent most of his career managing virtual communities. When he's not spending his time helping startups displace animals from the food supply chain, you'll find him hiking in Colorado, where he currently resides.

→ **If I were to visit Denver for a day, where should I go?**

Start your day off with a strong coffee or espresso at **Blue Sparrow Coffee** on Platte Street. From there, you are a short walk away from Commons Park downtown, which overlooks the Platte and Cherry Creek rivers. It's a great spot to see mountain and city views. I would then rent an electric bike—they are everywhere, so you can't miss them—and cycle along the Cherry Creek trail for brunch at **City, O' City** or **The Corner Beet**, which are both in the historic Capitol Hill neighborhood.

From there, consider a day-drinking tour through the RINO neighborhood, an afternoon baseball game at Coors Field, an immersive art experience at Meow Wolf, or get a ride to Red Rocks Amphitheater to see a show at the best outdoor music venue you'll ever visit. There is so much to do that covers good food, art, sports, and good people.

→ **What are your top five favorite places to eat?**

I can only name five? In no particular order:

Denver **Vegan Van**. Taco Bell, but better and vegan. Essentially the oldest vegan food business in town. When COVID hit, they started parking their food truck outside their house instead of downtown. On a sunny Saturday, their front lawn would be filled with purple-haired hippies eating vegan tostadas. It is truly magical.

Somebody People. This is truly a world-class restaurant with made-from-scratch Mediterranean fare and pasta. Every dish is amazing. I've spent so many days dreaming about their potatoes and secret-but-perfect tzatziki sauce. Their wine, cocktails, and shareable plates will blow anyone away, vegan or not. The best part may be the atmosphere. It's fun, they have DJs playing house music on the weekends, and there is a giant mural of David Bowie in one of the bathrooms. (*See* p. 80 for more info.)

Edgewater Market. There's a beautiful marketplace near the famous Sloan's Lake where you'll find two amazing vegan restaurants. Get juicy burgers from **Meta Burger** and a root vegetable Reuben sandwich from **Gladys Restaurant**.

Root Down. This restaurant is perfect if you have a mix of diet preferences in a group. It's a beautiful location overlooking the cityscape, and you can walk around afterward.

Himchuli. The best Indian and Nepali restaurant in Denver, and they have an all-vegan buffet once a month. You need this, just trust me.

→ **Tell me more about the work you do with Vevolution.**

Vevolution is the leading global network and investment marketplace for plant-based and cell-ag businesses. We're home to more than 4000 users, 1500 organizations, and nearly 500 investor members. Our marketplace makes it seamless to connect with our investor members, secure capital, and tap into the global ecosystem.

BLUE SPARROW COFFEE
1615 Platte Street, Suite 135
Denver, CO 80202

CITY, O' CITY
See p. 87

THE CORNER BEET
1401 N Ogden Street
Denver, CO 80218

VEGAN VAN
2760 Steele Street
Denver, CO 80205

SOMEBODY PEOPLE
See p. 80

META BURGER
See p. 83

GLADYS RESTAURANT
5505 W 20th Avenue,
Suite 116
Edgewater, CO 80214

ROOT DOWN
1600 W 33rd Avenue
Denver, CO 80211

HIMCHULI
3489 W 32nd Avenue
Denver, CO 80211

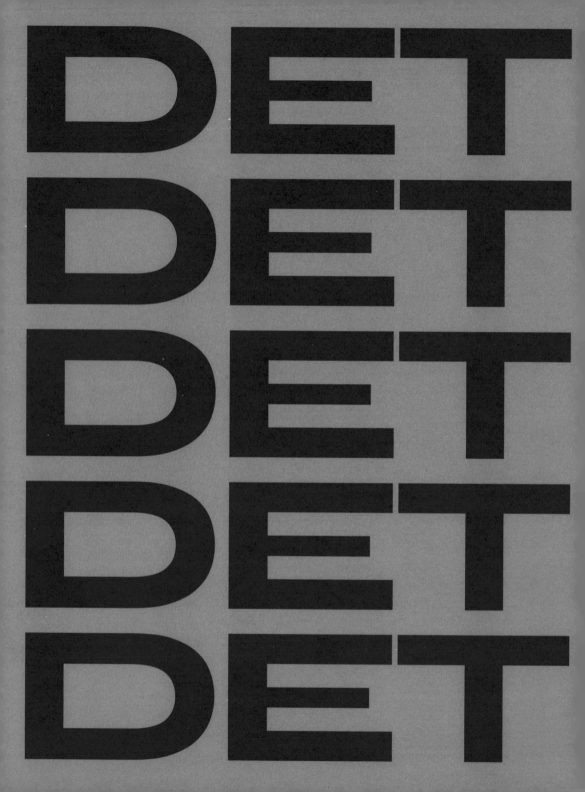

ROIT
ROIT
ROIT
ROIT
ROIT

Underpinned by the auto industry, Detroit (also known as Motor City and Motown) is a historically blue-collar city that's famous for being the original headquarters of Ford Motor Company. They set up shop more than a century ago, but the factory created a large number of jobs and acted as a catalyst for interstate migration. And as people from other parts of America came to Detroit for employment opportunities, they brought with them different cuisines and ethnicities, all of which are now part of Detroit's cultural makeup.

In the great culinary landscape, there are a few dishes Detroit is known for, like Coney Island hot dogs and their unique style of square, deep-dish pizza. At its worst, the food can be overly rich and stodgy, but more recently, there's been a broader shift toward lighter, veganized versions of soul food. We'll explore that in more detail in the pages to come.

A couple of must-dos when you're visiting the city:

Eastern Market: Saturday is the day to go to this fresh produce market. That's when the fruit and veggie suppliers are in the house, and you can more easily dodge shrapnel from the nearby meat shed.

Third Man Records: This record store is a compulsory stop for White Stripes fans since it's owned by the band's iconic frontman Jack White. You can browse books, clothing, records, turntables, and vinyl gear; check out new tunes in the listening booths; and even make your own DIY record at their in-store studio (although that doesn't always mean you should). For some reason, there's also an elephant scooter that rides around the store and accepts adult passengers. IYKYK.

DETROIT

EASTERN MARKET
(Open year-round from 6 a.m. to 4 p.m.)
1445 Adelaide Street
Detroit, MI 48207

THIRD MAN RECORDS
441 W Canfield Street
Detroit, MI 48201

CHILI MUSTARD ONIONS

VEGAN

→ **3411 BRUSH STREET
DETROIT, MI 48201**

When Pete LaCombe, chef-founder of Chili Mustard Onions (CMO), was in a car accident a few years back, he began to re-evaluate his life. Like many people who have had a health scare—whether it be due to an injury or illness—he decided that the only way forward was to go vegan, not just at a personal level, but through his work feeding others.

For Pete, this meant opening CMO, an ode to one of Detroit's true culinary masterpieces: the Coney dog. Now, if this is your first time traveling to Detroit, you might not be aware of what that is. So imagine a standard hot dog wedged between bun halves, then add chili, diced onions, and mustard. There you go: cultural phenomenon unlocked.

Usually a Coney dog is made from beef, but in CMO's case, they're bucking tradition by doing it animal-free, using Lightlife's Smart Dog wieners. I know some people take issue with soy-based meat alternatives, but as an ingredient, it remains one of the most functional and nutrient-rich sources of protein around. And whatever, it's tasty and it's not killing anything.

FOUNDER SPOTLIGHT

PETE LACOMBE

CHEF AND FOUNDER OF CHILI MUSTARD ONIONS

→ **How did CMO get started?**

My wife and I went vegan about nine years ago. I've been around food my entire life; always loved cooking, loved learning about it, was always around it. But when we went vegan, there wasn't anything we had grown up eating out here in Michigan. I missed a lot of food. And I really missed Coney dogs.

I wanted to take my passion for food, my knowledge, my palate, and create something plant-based that everyone would love, not just vegans. I opened up in Detroit, where the Coney dog started back in the early 1900s, and immediately got a lot of crap for it. People telling me to kill myself or that I wouldn't last a month
and every name in the book. The comments really got to me, but man, it also lit a fire under me that is still burning bright. I was on a mission at that point. I mean, I was already doing it for the animals, but when people start telling you you're going to fail, it gets you fired up. I'm a freak when it comes to that. It pushed me to hit it so hard from day one, and I never stopped.

We have a huge following—not just in Detroit but all over the world. People fly in and stop here first, coming in straight from the airport. We feed vegans, nonvegans, and those who are simply vegan curious. Every walk of life, nationality, religion ... people from everywhere. We've done it for almost three years now. We've even had rockstars and bands come through.

→ Any celeb customers whose names you can drop?

Wu-Tang was here every day during their stay in 2019. Loved it. They came for some Cannabis Cup thing. The guitarist from Queens of the Stone Age was in here a week ago. Anthrax, Rob Zombie, Blackberry Smoke, you name it.

→ What's going on in the kitchen?

I make everything here fresh each day. I don't open a can. I do use Beyond products, but I season it and make it my own. I do a "Whopper" that's better than a Burger King Whopper and a "Big Mac" that's better than a McDonald's Big Mac. I make an Arby's Beef 'N Cheddar out of seitan that would make you cry. It's all made and prepped in-house, so there's no cutting bags or pouring.

It's kind of comfort food. I use more organic ingredients than most restaurants. I have 20 different spices that I make, all organic. I use actual sea salt.

→ How do you handle the Coney dog purists?

I grew up in Detroit. You're going to get arguments that the Coney dog is from New York, but it's not; it's from Detroit. Been here since 1905. It goes back to Greek immigrants.

I want to ruffle some feathers. The ballsiest thing you can do in Detroit is open a vegan Coney dog place. But people love it now. I'm here, and I'm not going anywhere. If you're hungry, come on in. If you hate me, you don't know me.

DETROIT VEGAN SOUL

VEGAN | WOMAN-OWNED

→ **19614 GRAND RIVER AVENUE
DETROIT, MI 48223**

Detroit Vegan Soul is part of a growing number of Black-owned, vegan food establishments that are writing a new chapter of culinary tradition. It was founded in 2012 by Kirsten Ussery (general manager) and Erika Boyd (executive chef), who are determined to bring nourishing plant-based food to the community. After opening their initial location in West Village, the team was able to secure $125,000 in financing from the Entrepreneurs of Color Fund, which enabled them to open a second outpost. It's not only a testament to their success as business people, but to their ability to deliver a great-tasting meal.

First-timers should introduce themselves to the Detroit Vegan Soul menu by way of the Soul Platter, a sampling plate of mac and cheese, smoked collard greens with shitake, maple-glazed yams, and cornbread. If you're in for a second round, try the catfish tofu and meatballs (made from eggplant).

Their Grand River Avenue eatery is currently open Wednesday through Friday for online orders, pickup, and delivery (no dine in). There's also a weekly meal subscription service, catering, and freshly baked cakes (which can be shipped nationwide).

SEVA

VEGETARIAN | VEGAN OPTIONS AVAILABLE

→ **66 E FOREST AVENUE**
   DETROIT, MI 48201

At first glance, Seva looks like the kind of spot you'd go to with family or friends when you're searching for something uncomplicated and likely to please a crowd of fussy eaters. On closer inspection of the menu, this statement remains accurate. But you'll notice that everything on the menu also happens to be vegetarian or vegan.

Seva first opened in Midtown but, due to its popularity, has expanded to a second Detroit location. The secret to their success? They offer options, lots of them, that are familiar and recognizable. Perhaps that's why the restaurant has a reputation for winning over carnivores.

Straight out the gate we've got spinach and artichoke dip, chili cheese fries, bruschetta, and nacho dip on the appetizers list. It gives TGI Friday's, but without the corporate machinations or factory-farmed ingredients. The family-style thread continues throughout the dinner menu, with dishes like jambalaya, pad Thai, vegan mac, and asparagus ravioli that's available by the pan for carryout.

I'm a particular fan of the wine and beer offering, which takes up an equally dominant share of the menu space. If cocktails are your thing, you'll be pleased to find a short list of affordable classics, like margaritas, mojitos, and an Aperol spritz.

FREYA

VEGAN OPTIONS AVAILABLE

→ **2929 E GRAND BOULEVARD
DETROIT, MI 48202**

I've always been excited by vegan fine-dining menus. When a chef seriously puts their mind to it, the result can wind up far more interesting than the standard menu.

It's that level of ingenuity that draws me to a venue like Freya, a Scandinavian-style, tasting menu–only restaurant, where experience and atmosphere carry equal weight to the food.

There are only 12 tables on any given night, and as a diner, you need to go in open-minded. There's no a la carte menu to select from, so be ready to submit yourself to a culinary trust fall and allow the chefs to deliver their best work.

I'd set aside a good two to three hours for this kind of dinner event, so if patience is not your thing, look elsewhere. It can also take time to be seated, but I see that as an opportunity to enjoy a cocktail or wine before the show. FYI: there's a bar next door to tide you over.

Knowing how much consideration and effort goes into this style of dining, I find the $85 price tag to be ridiculously affordable. Be aware that prepayment is required when reserving a table— and before you get upset about that, know that this is often necessary so independent restaurants can survive. Between the high operational costs, notoriously low margins, and propensity for people to cancel at the last minute, charging at the time of reservation makes a lot of sense (and hey, airlines do it all the time). Furthermore, it allows the kitchen to minimize waste and order and prepare only the ingredients required that day.

Here's a tip: diners can choose from a selection of over 300 vinyl records to be played during their meal. So if you've got a penchant for Prince or Nipsey Hussle, they'll bring the beats.

PIE-SCI PIZZA

VEGAN OPTIONS AVAILABLE

→ **5163 TRUMBULL AVENUE
WOODBRIDGE, DETROIT, MI 48208**

This pizza-science lab has no time for the confines of tradition. Pizza fundamentalists may argue over the superiority of an Italian thin and crispy base over the stodgy stylings of Chicago deep dish, and the appropriate ratio of toppings to crust. But these pie-sci pizza nerds are embracing experimentation with reckless abandon.

Ingredients like tofu bacon, vegan chicken, TVP, jackfruit, seitan, and cashew-based cheese are warmly embraced here, and most menu items can be ordered vegan and/or gluten-free. There's even a vegan herb mayo available for dipping your pizza crusts into. It really is these little details that make a venue special.

When dine-in restaurants closed in 2020, Pie-Sci was able to pivot to curbside pickup and quickly became inundated with customers, many of whom probably would have perished from starvation during the lockdown had they been required to cook for themselves. Further proof that when the economy takes a turn for the worse, true innovation tends to thrive.

Of note: Pie-Sci Pizza is known for a monstrous mashup called the "pizzagna." I haven't tried it, but I'm sure they'd be willing to veganize it if you wanted to give it a stab.

KANSA
KANSA
KANSA
KANSA
KANSA

S CITY

S CITY

S CITY

S CITY

S CITY

Otherwise known as Cowtown for its prolific BBQ culture, Kansas City hasn't been as progressive as other parts of the country when it comes to embracing a plant-forward lifestyle. But no matter how entrenched animal agriculture might be in the city's history, it's unable to stop the swelling demand for plant-based options. In fact, an increasing number of "meateries" are now offering vegan or vegetarian alternatives:

Char Bar serves jackfruit-and-cauliflower-based alternatives alongside its meat-heavy menu.

Joe's Kansas City Bar-B-Que, located in a gas station, offers its classic Z-Man burger made with portobello mushroom instead of meat.

Jazzy B's Diner also serves portobello mushroom alternatives in place of classic beef burgers and tacos.

Look, you're not going to find as many vegan restaurants per capita as you'd expect in a city like LA or NYC. But you won't starve. And what KC lacks in foodie options, it makes up for in transport score and all-round livability. For instance, its free Streetcar service operates from early morning to late night, zipping along a 2.2-mile drag from Downtown to Union Station. That's going to get you to most major tourist hotspots, including the Crossroads Arts District, Central Business District, and City Market. Plus, it's got free Wi-Fi on board so you can look up restaurant menus and Yelp reviews while you ride.

My tip for the artsy folk: Head to the Crossroads District first. That's where you'll find breweries, boutiques, and spritzy little jazz bars for a naughty night on the town.

KANSAS CITY

CHAR BAR
4050 Pennsylvania Avenue
Kansas City, MO 64111

JOE'S KANSAS CITY BAR-B-QUE
3002 W 47th Avenue
Kansas City, KS 66103

JAZZY B'S DINER
316 SE Douglas Street
Lee's Summit, MO 64063

PIRATE'S BONE BURGERS

VEGAN

→ **2000 MAIN STREET
KANSAS CITY, MO 64108**

They do two things at Pirate's Bone Burgers, and they do them well.

On one side, you've got burgers. And to appeal to those who enjoy the simple life, there's an Impossible patty tucked tightly between leafy greens, pickles, and a classic bun. Or if you want to spice things up, try adding chipotle aioli and a second patty. Or go wild and order the MacRibless or their fried "chix" burger.

On the other side of the menu, there's fries that are handmade daily so you know these guys aren't fooling around when it comes to potatoes. Ordering instructions are simple: choose your size (small or large) and your seasoning (Cajun, truffle, herb, BBQ, or buffalo), and you're set. Simple yet satisfying.

I can't explain what pirates or bones have to do with the menu, but it's best not to overthink it. It's burgers, and they're plant-based and yummy.

GIGI'S VEGAN + WELLNESS CAFÉ

VEGAN | WOMAN-OWNED

→ **1103 WESTPORT ROAD
KANSAS CITY, MO 64111**

Gigi Jones is a pioneer of the Kansas City vegan community. In 2015, a cancer diagnosis prompted her to re-evaluate her diet and lifestyle and ultimately go vegan. It was a life-changing—if not life-saving—decision.

Now a personal health coach, Gigi is helping others discover the benefits of plant-based eating at her vegan and wellness cafe, where everything is clean, fresh, and doesn't leave you feeling like you've been socked in the gut with a wet sea bass. I'm talking raw salads, cold-pressed juices and smoothies, wraps, and kale on everything. Seriously, there's a tremendous amount of kale going on here (Gigi even has her own kale chip product line, which was featured on *Shark Tank* in 2021). It's all a bit healthy for me, but perfect for those who want to nourish their bodies between yoga sessions.

Gigi also offers a customized meal prep service. It's super flexible, so there's no need to worry about lock-in contracts (it's not Verizon), and it provides three solid meals a day for a set period of your choosing. Specific dietary requests, such as low inflammation, gluten-free, diabetic, and kid-friendly, are all welcomed, which is refreshing for anyone living with dietary restrictions.

5 MINUTES WITH

GIGI JONES
OWNER OF GIGI'S VEGAN + WELLNESS CAFÉ

→ **Gigi, tell us about Gigi's.**

Our cafe is for people looking for healthy alternatives and plant-based living. In addition to meals, we offer minerals and supplements and support our patrons through health coaching and cooking classes.

→ **What's your most popular dish?**

The Kale Yeah bowl (or wrap)! We're known for creating a lot of dishes with kale ... which we love because it's a superfood. In fact, we serve all our meals with sprouts and microgreens because the chlorophyll and enzymes they contain are so beneficial to the body. Our juices are quite popular too; they're cold-pressed, organic, and made in-house along with our milks.

We don't fry any of our food here, and everything is soy-and gluten-free. But don't get me wrong, this isn't a place where people take a look at the menu and go, "Oh no, there's no salt or sugar." It's possible to find healthier substitutes that still taste good.

→ **Have any insider tips on what to do in Kansas City?**

We are the organizers of the Midwest Soul Vegfest, which is usually held in October at the end of each harvest. We bring speakers in from all over and get people familiar with eating healthy and changing their lifestyles. It's been especially important for the African American community throughout COVID; at a time like this, we don't want people to be afraid of vegetables.

→ Why did you choose the Westport neighborhood to set up your business?

People look at our location and say, "You chose Westport? Why did you choose Westport?" But I feel like Westport chose me. Being able to create something like this in an area that has so much history is just amazing to me. I'm really excited to have a concept like Gigi's in the neighborhood, a place where we can grow our own food and have a garden at the back of the cafe. And if we can't grow something ourselves, we have close access to local community farmers. We even go and pick strawberries from a local farm and have them on our menu that day.

NOTE

If you're keen to go berry picking like Gigi, try **Wohletz Farm Fresh** or **Gieringers**. Both are open to the public during the strawberry, blackberry, and blueberry seasons.

WOHLETZ FARM FRESH
1831 N 1100 Road
Lawrence, KS 66046

GIERINGERS
39345 W 183rd Street
Edgerton, KS 66021

MUD PIE BAKERY & COFFEEHOUSE

VEGAN

→ **7319 W 95TH STREET**
OVERLAND PARK, KS 66212

When Ashley and Michael Valverde opened their coffee shop
and bakehouse back in 2011, veganism was not in vogue. There
was nothing like it in Kansas City at the time, which to some was
a signal of opportunity, and to others, a lack thereof. And without
any experience in the field of hospitality, the odds of entrepreneurial
success were not stacked in the couple's favor. But the best startup
founders are willing to take a gamble, and in the case of the Valverdes,
their business bravery has paid off.

Twelve years after opening, Mud Pie Bakery & Coffeehouse is
still going strong, serving hot beverages and vegan baked treats all
day long, plus a couple of special cupcake flavors on rotation daily.
Not only are the pastries made from scratch using fully animal-free
ingredients, the plant-based milks are all made in-house too.

For their first three years of business, Ashley's mother took
on the role of cake decorator/nonvegan in residence, testing the
bakery's plant-based recipes against their traditional counterparts.
Having that objective feedback allowed the team to better meet
customers' expectations of taste and ultimately cater to people
of all dietary persuasions.

Over time, community awareness around the vegan diet and its
benefits has grown, as have the number of businesses catering to
a vegan lifestyle. But it's not an all-or-nothing approach. According
to Michael, "Our whole goal is to bring in people who might not even
be vegetarian ... and show them that plant-based food can be very
good." After 12 years in business, I'd say that's not just a goal for
them anymore; it's an achievement.

5 MINUTES WITH

MICHAEL VALVERDE

CO-OWNER OF MUD PIE BAKERY & COFFEEHOUSE

→ **Considering you'd never worked in hospitality before, what drove you and your wife Ashley to open a cafe?**

As vegans, we wanted to set up a coffee shop where everything on the menu was something we could order. We wanted to show people that it's not hard to be vegan.

→ **There's a lot of debate around labels these days, whether it's vegan, plant-based, or animal-free. What's your take on the lingo?**

Twelve years ago, *vegan* was kind of a bad word; it was very polarizing. We've considered switching to the term *plant-based*, which people seem more open to. But at the same time, we're used to the criticism around the term *vegan* ... so we figured screw it, let's keep it. That's how people know us, and we've embraced it.

→ **How did COVID impact your business?**

A lot. Prior to the pandemic, we employed over 30 people, and that felt like a big achievement for us, being in a position to create those jobs. But when COVID hit, we were forced to cut back on staff, around 20 people, maybe more. We really tried to help them the best we could. As the pandemic continued, we reached a point where we had to either reopen the business to keep it afloat and bring the team back or close operations for good.

By then, people were nervous about coming back to work. Most didn't … maybe only three or four people returned. That was difficult, but ultimately, it's about their comfort level. They're the ones here every day, and we respect that.

→ **Where else do you recommend for a great plant-based meal in Kansas City?**

The Fix! is a favorite. My friend David Schwartz owns it, and the place is killer. There's many places here that are not exclusively plant-based but have a decent range of options, so I wouldn't discount those either.

You know, when we were the only vegan place in town, I used to feel very competitive. I don't know why, but that's changed now. There's more plant-based businesses here these days, and I have more friends in the community, so I've chilled out a bit. After all, we're all on the same team.

THE FIX!
600 E 31st Street
Kansas City, MO 64109

LAS V
LAS V
LAS V
LAS V
LAS V

GAS
GAS
GAS
GAS
GAS

LAS VEGAS

When I think of Las Vegas, I imagine a labyrinth of casinos, flashing neon lights, and the plotline of *The Hangover* (or a myriad similar romping comedies set in the haze of Sin City). But its buoyant plant-based food scene is never the first thing that comes to mind. So you might be surprised to learn that Las Vegas is actually a hotspot of healthy delectables.

It makes sense when you think about it, though. Just consider the sheer volume of tourists who pass through the desert corridor each week, loaded with cash to lose. Those people need sustenance, and oftentimes, they'll want it in a form that's free from animal products (just like they do back home).

A large number of Vegas's luxury hotel restaurants now offer veganized menus, which to me is a major sign that consumer demand is shifting in the right direction. If you have the budget to back it up, I'd recommend checking out **Wynn Las Vegas and Encore Resort**, where every restaurant on location offers vegan options. Another spot at the top of my list is **The Venetian**, which offers a wide range of eateries that cater to those of a plant-based persuasion.

Even traditional steakhouses are getting in on the game here. Take **Bouchon**, for instance, the high-end concept by Thomas Keller. It has an off-menu "Vegan Chop" that is available for those who prefer their meat made from mushrooms. In fact, the city is inundated with celebrity chef dining concepts, and while you'll pay a premium, you can expect that most of these venues will cater to vegan and vegetarian diners with ease.

There's even a dedicated vegan grocery store, **Veg-In-Out Market** (see opposite), that's stocked with everything, from big-name brands to local provedores.

A word of warning to those with an entrepreneurial spirit: the name Viva Las Vegan has already been taken by a New Orleans food truck. Consider my trademark application abandoned.

WYNN LAS VEGAS & ENCORE RESORT
3131 Las Vegas Boulevard S
Las Vegas, NV 89109

THE VENETIAN LAS VEGAS (BOUCHON LOCATED ON 10TH FLOOR)
3355 S Las Vegas Boulevard
Las Vegas, NV 89101

OTHER WAYS TO SPEND YOUR $$$ IN VEGAS

VEG-IN-OUT MARKET

→ **2301 E SUNSET ROAD LAS VEGAS, NV 89119**

This spot made headlines when it opened in late 2019 as Vegas's first vegan grocery store. You can't buy fresh produce here, but you can find an enormous range of pantry, snack, and frozen goodies—all of which have passed the "approved ingredients" test. So you can relax on the label scrutiny for just a moment.

Side note: the market is also a major supporter of the Las Vegan Food Bank, a volunteer organization providing vegan food boxes to anyone requiring assistance. Shoppers are encouraged to get involved by donating non-perishable items to the store's dedicated drop-off zone. In return, they're entered in a monthly prize pack drawing (not that an incentive was needed to support the cause!).

For fresh produce, pickles, and chutneys, there's a collection of **LAS VEGAS FARMERS' MARKETS** that operate at multiple locations on weekly and monthly schedules. Check their website for the latest seasonal market hours. lasvegasfarmersmarket.com

VINTAGE VEGAN DINER

WOMAN-OWNED

→ **1370 W CHEYENNE AVENUE NORTH LAS VEGAS, NV 89030**

Vintage Vegan Diner opened in May 2020 during Armageddon, which is a bold move for some, but owners Tumn and Taylor have a reputation for living outside of their comfort zones. (They recently converted their van into a permanent home on wheels. You can follow the wild ride on IG @TumnandTay.)

This is not an actual restaurant diner; it's a range of frozen, heat-and-eat snacks created by the adventurous duo. Right now, the Vintage Vegan Diner range includes cookie dough, sliders, and breaded tofu bites (before you complain that tofu is tasteless, these puppies come in flavors like buffalo, BBQ, and lemon pepper). And forget the rigmarole of traditional grocery checkouts; the products are dispensed from a vegan vending machine on location at Ferguson's Downtown Las Vegas. I can assure you, it's difficult to miss considering the brand's baby pink and blue packaging is so ICONIC. But then again, I'm a sucker for the retro '50s aesthetic.

Major grocery stores include **NATURAL GROCERS, SPROUTS, WHOLE FOODS,** and **TRADER JOE'S**, and although their selection of vegan items isn't as extensive as in larger cities, your favorite brands of tempeh and oat milk should still be covered.

121

VEGGY STREET

VEGAN

→ **1110 E SILVERADO RANCH BOULEVARD #100
LAS VEGAS, NV 89183**

→ **5135 S FORT APACHE ROAD,
SUITE 110
LAS VEGAS, NV 89148**

There can never be enough burger restaurants. And you can't convince me otherwise.

Veggy Street has opted for the gold standard in beef analogues: the Beyond patty, which, in my opinion, provides a pretty authentic burger experience. These sizzling little slabs are sandwiched between pretzel buns and adorned with a suspiciously healthy-looking serving of salad ingredients. This varies depending on your fancy, but expect cabbage, avocado, and caramelized onions as well as the usual lettuce and tomato options.

If you're undergoing burger fatigue, try the Co Sheen Ya instead. These little croquettes are based on a Brazilian street food called *coxinha* (pronounced co-sheen-ya), which are traditionally made from chicken and cream cheese. Veggy Street's version is fully veganized but equally tasty. Because let's be honest, fried things are always more delicious, and there's no shame in admitting that.

TARANTINO'S VEGAN

VEGAN

→ **7960 S RAINBOW BOULEVARD,
SUITE 8000G
LAS VEGAS, NV 89139**

I originally thought this was going to be a Quentin Tarantino–themed restaurant—a garish diner with booths, a dance floor, and Uma Thurman out back exacting revenge on someone, perhaps the mastermind responsible for factory farming.

But Tarantino's Vegan is a different place. It's actually a family-run Italian restaurant serving plant-powered versions of the classics.

If you're a pasta person, the choices are simple but solid:

1. Choose your base structure (spaghetti, angel hair, rigatoni, zucchini noodles, and more).

2. Select a sauce (spicy tomato, pesto, alfredo, bolognese ... they're all here).

3. Finally, add your enhancements (much like adding custom pizza toppings, with ingredients like capers, artichoke hearts, basil, olives, and mushrooms).

Make sure your dining companion orders something different so you can eat from their plate too. That's my strategy. Tell them to try the antipasto platter, stuffed portobello mushrooms, calzone, or chick'n parm. I don't know if it's their subtle branding, lack of greenwashing, or the fact that Italian food is delicious regardless of meat and dairy's involvement, but it's easy to forget that "vegan" is part of the Tarantino's name.

CHIKYŪ VEGAN SUSHI BAR

VEGAN

→ **1740 E SERENE AVENUE #130
LAS VEGAS, NV 89123**

Vegas isn't known for its elegant Japanese cuisine, but maybe it's because the locals are so good at keeping secrets. After all, what happens in Vegas stays ... vegan.

Compared to the glaring neon light show that is the Strip, Chikyū is a calming contrast. This fully plant-based sushi bar and izakaya celebrates vegetables, roots, flowers, and seaweeds rather than glorifying meat. Apart from that crucial point of difference, the menu is based on traditional Japanese flavors, techniques, and dishes, such as ramen, tempura, nigiri, and (sushi) rolls.

What really struck me, however, was their "Euphorics" menu, a short selection of beverages that use mood-enhancing nootropics instead of alcohol. Definitely don't leave without trying one. It may improve your cognitive abilities and decision-making skills as the night wears on and the casino lights call.

TARANTINO'S VEGAN (*see* p. 123)

VEG-IN-OUT MARKET (*see* p. 121)

TACOTARIAN (*see* p. 132)

CHIKYŪ VEGAN SUSHI BAR (*see* p. 125)

TACO DIVE BAR

VEGAN

→ **4080 PARADISE ROAD
LAS VEGAS, NV 89169**

In one sense, Taco Dive Bar is brutally up front about who they are and what they do. There's no mistaking that if you go here, you're going to get booze, mismatched seating, a bit of video poker, and probably a hangover.

On the other hand, they're cheekily deceptive. Nothing about the neon lights or graffiti-scrawled walls points to the fact that Taco Dive Bar is actually a vegan restaurant. I find it endearing. And I'm going to bet you that half the tourists who wander into this joint never even realize that their taco was an animal-free alternative.

They've got your White Claws covered (in case you didn't pregame before heading out on the town), a decent selection of beers, and a short list of cocktails, all sticking to the venue's theme. Snacks are kept simple, with plenty of stuffed tortillas, nachos, and fries, all topped with a choice of spiced-up proteins, sauces, and slaws. FYI: for those traveling to the US for the first time, a "Garbage Bag" is a small bag of Frito chips torn open and slathered with typical nacho toppings (in this case queso, pico de gallo, and sour cream).

Every crevice of the space is splattered with street art, but if that's not enough for your visual entertainment, they've got gaming stations built into the bar top. With video poker, keno, and a 24/7 happy hour, it's a clever AF play on the City of Sin, but it's more of a reference to their surroundings than the core of Taco Dive Bar's identity—which I like to think of as "Vegan by Stealth."

CHEF KENNY'S ASIAN VEGAN RESTAURANT

VEGAN

→ **6820 SPRING MOUNTAIN ROAD
LAS VEGAS, NV 89146**

I always get excited about vegetarian or vegan Asian cuisine and its ability to use meat-free alternatives without missing a beat on flavor. It's often an easy win when you're trying to coax an omnivore to the table without using a pork chop as bait.

At Chef Kenny's place, I'd ease them in with sushi to start. Unlike typical restaurants where vegan sushi options are limited to rice with a pop of avocado on top, Chef's has vegan tuna, salmon, and even eel on the go. They offer rainbow, crunchy jackfruit, vegan California, and my favorite, the Sexy roll. I haven't tried it, but I feel like I'd like it.

Beyond that, you'd do well ordering any of the specialty dishes. Something like spicy kung pao beef or veggie Mongolian beef is likely to satisfy a meat lover, and if I wasn't concerned about feeding their bloodlust for meat-like substances, I might venture into a classic bean curd dish, like Buddha's Delight. Add some sauteed Chinese broccoli and you can't go wrong (come on, everyone loves that, whether they're vegan or not).

I think Western culture tends to forget that products like soy chicken and konjac shrimp have been used by Asian restaurants long before Silicon Valley's alt-protein hype began. It's true that some people aren't down with it, and that's fair. But many of us still crave a chunk of protein to chew on, so pro tip for the newbies: if you are partial to mock-meats, know that you can often find them for cheap in the freezer section of Asian grocery stores. You can also hit up the pantry section for dried soy protein hunks and canned vegan pork, chicken, and duck. They're often no different from what's being sold at four times the price at upmarket retailers.

RONALD'S DONUTS

VEGAN OPTIONS AVAILABLE

→ **4600 SPRING MOUNTAIN ROAD
LAS VEGAS, NV 89102**

I get an odd sense of nostalgia when I walk through the Ronald's parking lot. It's unremarkable; the squat brick storefront could easily be mistaken for the dry cleaner I used to visit as a kid when I'd accompany my mom on her errands runs. Although it's literally on the other side of the world from where I grew up in Australia, it feels just like a Chinatown strip mall we'd visit back home. There's a psychic next door, an immigration lawyer, and an AT&T outlet. Cars blur past with their engines roaring. And if it weren't for the big red "DONUTS" sign overhead, I probably would have walked straight past it.

Ronald's Donuts is the reason travel guides like this exist. It's the kind of place that's so unassuming that, unless you'd been given a hot tip and a map with local coordinates, you'd never think to go there. At least not to find some of the best vegan donuts in the country. This place is a genuine local treasure, so if you've had the good fortune of discovering it, here's my advice on how to optimize the experience.

1. You're working with a cash-only operation here, so come prepared.

2. Most of the donuts are vegan, but they're not clearly labeled. It's best to ask the staff which is which.

3. Leave your phone in your pocket; there are no Instagrammable gimmicks going on here. No unicorn donuts, rainbow BS, or concoctions piled high with oreos and fairy dust. Just straight up, classic, fried dough puffs.

4. The shop is open 24 hours a day. You may be tempted to visit twice in a 24-hour period. You will not be the first to do such a thing, and you won't be the last.

5. It's fair to assume that nobody has ever bought a donut from Ronald's and walked away disappointed, thinking, "Man this is nice, but I wish they'd put dairy in it."

I know it can be frustrating when businesses don't put up flashing lights or hire a live brass band to announce their excellent vegan options. But I kinda like the fact that Ronald's doesn't feel the need to promote it. Their reputation rests on having the best donuts in Las Vegas, full stop.

TACOTARIAN

VEGAN

→ **1130 S CASINO CENTER BOULEVARD #170
LAS VEGAS, NV 89104**

The founders of Tacotarian understand that there's more to restaurants than the food itself. In order to create an experience that people want to keep coming back to, there needs to be a story behind it. An actual connection to the people who put their time (and most likely sweat and tears) into making the food, shaping the space, and managing all those little unseen details that we never consider as customers.

The Tacotarian team does this really well. Carlos, Kirsten, Regina, and Dan came up with the concept in 2018 after a stint in Mexico City, where they were inspired—if not a little surprised—by the availability of plant-based options. With a wealth of hospitality and entrepreneurial experience behind them, the quartet decided to bring some of that flavor to Las Vegas and open the city's first dedicated, plant-based taco emporium.

Seriously, this place has a huge taco menu, and it absolutely slaps. These handheld flavor boats go well beyond the basics, incorporating ingredients like plantains, traditional mole sauce, hibiscus flower, fried beer-battered avocado, mashed potatoes, and chili-braised jackfruit. For those who just discovered birria on TikTok a while back, I'd suggest getting your hands on the Tacotarian version, which is made of a Beyond Meat and jackfruit blend with a dipping sauce that you'll definitely make a mess with. Just resign yourself to it; you're not at the Met Gala right now. It's OK to get your hands dirty.

As someone who's married to my business cofounder, I enjoy seeing two married couples work together. I know some people would consider that a fast road to divorce, and I completely get it. But when your vision is aligned and you're working toward the same goal, there's nothing like sharing the journey (and your successes) with your partner.

UNDERGROUND INTEL

The Tacotarian team also operates a slick delivery/pickup-only operation called Underground Burgers. It came about through the challenges of pandemic dining, when comforting plant-based options were hard to come by. But armed with Impossible patties and their own secret sauce, these guys rose to the occasion, creating a short fast-food-style menu for rapid burger deployment.

Delivery details are on their website, or you can pick up your burgers, fries, and vanilla coconut shakes in person at their DTLV location.

EATUNDERGROUNDBURGER.COM

LOS AN
LOS AN
LOS AN
LOS AN
LOS AN

GELES
GELES
GELES
GELES
GELES

LOS ANGELES

Arguably the vegan capital of the United States, Los Angeles is a city saturated with celebrities, sunshine, and the constant judgmental glare of my neighbor who's always on a juice cleanse and doing power squats on the front lawn. LA people are so serious about their plant-powered meals, I wouldn't be surprised if my next vegan burger was blessed and delivered by Joaquin Phoenix himself.

I remember the first time I visited. My Uber was searing down Sunset Boulevard, both sides studded with the iconic palm trees I'd seen in movies. I looked out the window at the ostentatious Hollywood Hills homes on the right and massive billboards promoting new Netflix shows on the left. It looked exactly as I'd imagined it ... like walking through my television and into this alternate universe.

What struck me was how old things looked; amidst the new high-rise developments, the streets still look like a snapshot of the 1960s. Slightly run-down diners, auto repair shops and strip malls with retro signage, vintage Spanish villas, houses on stilts, and architectural designs that look as though they were commissioned by the Jetsons. Then there's the juxtaposition between obscene wealth and poverty, which is both fascinating and heartbreaking to witness so blatantly, at least for a country so prosperous.

I was drawn to LA and its eccentricities as soon as I got there. In fact, it's where I live now, on the same block Marilyn Monroe and Frank Sinatra once resided. But it wasn't just the culture of extremes or the persistently pleasant weather that won me over. It was because I was launching my own plant-based company. And if there's anywhere in America where clean-eating, yoga-posing, vegan food fanatics thrive, it's Los Angeles.

LA isn't known for fine dining. I'll admit, I've struggled to find a mind-blowing Michelin star experience here (I'm not saying it doesn't exist; it's just much harder to come by). But what LA excels in is street food (taco trucks and plant-based burger pop-ups are a constant) and fresh, fast, and casual restaurants.

I'm not going to suggest the typical tourist stops here; you can Google them or find them on any tourist site. Instead, here are my tips on what to check out when you visit.

- **Runyon Canyon dog park**. Even if you don't have a dog, go here. It's heaven to see their slobbering, smiling faces as they romp around in the sand, chasing balls and sniffing each other's butts.

- Comedy clubs like **The Groundlings, The Comedy Store**, and **Laugh Factory**. It's not uncommon to see celebs test out their new material on a school night, for the price of a couple of drinks.

- **Beverly Hills**. Sometimes I'll just hop in my rattling Prius and drive around the estates to ogle at the lashings of luxury. Is that massive building with the pristine green lawn a hotel? An entire apartment complex? No, it's just one of Adele's mansions.

Visit one of the many food markets, like **Grand Central Market** (there's a bunch of vegan options to choose from here, but you're mainly coming for the atmosphere), **Smorgasburg LA** (open every Sunday), or **Vegan Street Fair**, which is held on various weekends throughout the year in North Hollywood.

**RUNYON CANYON
DOG PARK**
2000 N Fuller Avenue
Los Angeles, CA 90046

THE GROUNDLINGS
7307 Melrose Avenue
Los Angeles, CA 90046

THE COMEDY STORE
8433 Sunset Boulevard
Los Angeles, CA 90069

LAUGH FACTORY
8001 Sunset Boulevard
Los Angeles, CA 90046

GRAND CENTRAL MARKET
317 S Broadway
Los Angeles, CA 90013

SMORGASBURG LA
777 S Alameda Street
Los Angeles, CA 90021

VEGAN STREET FAIR
11223 Chandler Boulevard
(between Tujunga & Vineland)
North Hollywood, CA 91601

SAGE PLANT BASED BISTRO

VEGAN

→ **4130 SEPULVEDA BOULEVARD CULVER CITY, CA 90230**

On the surface, it looks like a typical gastropub. You'll recognize the long communal tables lined with those metal chairs that—at one point—were a compulsory component of every trendy cafe on the planet. I think this sense of familiarity works in Sage's favor because it helps attract a broader audience of patrons who might not otherwise consider a plant-based restaurant. Getting people over the line and through the door is always the hardest part. But once there, I doubt anyone would be disappointed.

The menu has everything you'd expect from a vegan establishment: cauliflower wings, tacos, nachos, pizza, big salads, burritos, and bowls. Standouts for me, however, are the fresh-baked soft pretzels and the veggie-heavy pizzas—all of which can be made gluten-free. I'm particularly excited about the inclusion of mac and cheese and BBQ-pineapple pizzas on the menu. Bold. Controversial. I like it.

A lot of businesses talk shit these days; they throw a few buzzwords like "sustainability" and "save the earth" on their website and call it a day. But Sage doesn't take this lazy, green-washed approach. Rather, the restaurant is committed to offering transparency regarding their supply chain and business practices, and that's evident in every interaction I've had with them, from the venue itself to their website.

As a result, they're big on regenerative agricultural practices, and they intentionally work with farmers who follow its principles. Regenerative farming has tremendous potential for addressing climate change, as it seeks to remove carbon from the atmosphere and create carbon-rich, fertile soil. That's a good thing! Once upon a time, America's grasslands would suck carbon out of the air and store it underground in the soil. But modern farming methods—developed for maximum efficiency at all costs—have led to this carbon being released back into the atmosphere instead. Regenerative agriculture aims to fix that by sequestering that nastiness out of the air and burying it like nature intended.

There's four Sage Plant Based Bistro locations in LA, including one in Echo Park that doubles as a brewery and is run by some rad ladies. To discover the other locations, visit sageveganbistro.com.

KISS
-the-
GROUND.

Farmhouse Ale w/ honey, orange peel,
charred lemon & lemon verbena

16 FL. OZ. | ABV 5.7%

PORTION OF PROCEEDS GO TO KISS THE GROUND
Kisstheground.com

5 MINUTES WITH

ELYSABETH ALFANO

COFOUNDER AND CEO OF VEGTECH™ INVEST, HOST OF *THE PLANTBASED BUSINESS HOUR* PODCAST

Elysabeth is a powerhouse. When we first moved to the States, I would watch her *Plantbased Business Hour* interviews and imagine being one of her guests at the forefront of food tech (I've since had my own episode!). She is the CEO of VegTech™ Invest, as well as a writer, public speaker, consultant, and all-around expert in the plant-based industry and the intersection of sustainability and our global food supply system.

→ **Tell us a little bit about the work you do with VegTech and The *Plantbased Business Hour*.**

As the CEO of VegTech™ Invest, along with my partner Dr. Sasha Goodman, we created and currently advise the world's first Plant-based Innovation and Climate ETF (Exchange Traded Fund), EATV. EATV invests in public companies that are innovating with plants and plant-derived ingredients to create animal-free products for sustainable consumption, thus addressing climate change and food insecurity.

On *The Plantbased Business Hour*, I interview the thought leaders, CEOs, entrepreneurs, scientists, and analysts who are launching new plant-based initiatives in a shifting global food supply system, away from inefficient animal products.

→ **How has the plant-based industry changed since you first started working in this space?**

There are so many more products now, and the marketing has finally splintered. Long gone are the days of saying you are plant-based and hoping that is enough. Are you plant-based for mothers who want their children to be healthy or for older people who are trying to bring down their cholesterol? Are you doing it for Gen Z, which cares about the planet or animal lovers who are serious about loving animals? The sector is large enough that you can market to specific portions of it and have a very strong business model. And brand authenticity is everything.

→ **You split your time between Chicago and LA. Which restaurants do you miss the most whenever you're out of town?**

Oh, how I love **Plant Food + Wine** on Abbott Kinney in Venice in LA. I also love **Au Lac** downtown; the octopus dish is the bomb! **Vinh Loi** is super good, but a bit far away from the heart of LA. I can't eat at **Crossroads**, **Pura Vita**, or **Nic's on Beverly** enough. **Double Zero** is dangerous.

I do love Althea in Chicago. I can't keep myself from Sam & Gertie's and Ka'lish. I love Bloom in Wicker Park, and the vegan menu at Brass Heart is off the charts. Off the charts! Upton's Breakroom is pretty amazing, and you have to go to The Chicago Diner and Soul City Veg for history!

see over

→ Do you have any local shopping tips for someone who loves to cook at home?

Start with what you know. You like guacamole? Make guacamole and get that under your belt. You like tacos? Start there. Don't overthink it!

Invest in spices! Much of cooking is in the seasonings, so don't be shy.

Stop psyching yourself out. Start with simple recipes or just fool around in the kitchen. Get familiar with your own kitchen and taste buds and build from there. And don't imagine you won't like it because YOU JUST MIGHT!

I used to have yogurt every morning, and I couldn't imagine going without it. Then I thought, *This is stupid. I am not going to not go vegan because of yogurt or cheese? I can get past this.* So, I figured tofu is white, and yogurt is white. I will just replace yogurt with tofu and see what happens. I now make the following every morning: ⅓ a container of drained tofu, 1 tablespoon of hemp seeds, ½ cup of berries, ½ cup of raw oats, and 1 tablespoon of date syrup. 375 calories. 17.5 grams of protein. Gobs of fiber, ready in less than five minutes. It's both filling and delicious! So don't tell me you can't be vegan. I got over yogurt and cheese, and you can too (if you want to).

Also buy a pair of scissors and keep them in the kitchen. Best kitchen tool ever.

Stay up to date with the latest *Plantbased Business Hour* episodes by subscribing on iTunes or Spotify. For more about Elysabeth and some cracking recipes, visit elysabethalfano.com.

PLANT FOOD + WINE
1009 Abbot Kinney Boulevard
Venice, CA 90291

AU LAC
710 W First Street
Los Angeles, CA 90012

VINH LOI TOFU
11818 South Street, Suite 101
Cerritos, CA 90703

CROSSROADS KITCHEN
See p. 144

PURA VITA
See p. 149

NIC'S ON BEVERLY
See p. 152

DOUBLE ZERO
See p. 155

ELYSABETH'S AVOCADO, BANANA, AND SWEET POTATO SMOOTHIE BOWL

SERVES 1

½ sweet potato, baked, skin removed

½ avocado

1 small ripe banana

½ cup plant-based yogurt or non-dairy milk (optional)

Optional toppings: coconut flakes, hemp seeds, diced dates

Combine ingredients together in a blender and blitz until smooth and creamy.

Pour in a bowl and add coconut flakes, hemp seeds, and diced dates. For a heartier option, blend with raw oats and date syrup to sweeten it up. Enjoy!

CROSSROADS KITCHEN

VEGAN

→ **8284 MELROSE AVENUE**
LOS ANGELES, CA 90046

Ask any local about the best vegan restaurants in LA, and chances are they'll mention Crossroads. Then they'll quickly add that "it's not cheap," which is an accurate observation.

That's not to say it's expensive, though. Considering the amount of work that goes into operating—for lack of a better term—a more "upmarket" restaurant, I'd say diners are getting a sweet deal at Crossroads. Sure, you won't find the same ambience of adrenaline, honking cars, and occasional gunshot noises that you might experience at an LA food truck. But you will buckle in for a thoughtful and well-executed meal.

Having married a chef whose own restaurant boasted an 18-course, blind tasting menu and an excessive amount of gastronomical showmanship, I've spent the last few years fatigued by this endless procession of tiny plates. As a result, I've found myself swinging to the opposite side of the culinary spectrum, with a freezer full of frozen pizza bases and an arthritic condition in my fingers caused by excessive UberEats usage.

But the tasting menu at Crossroads Kitchen has me excited again. I'm intrigued by the ingredients and how the chefs navigate any perceived limitations of a meat- and dairy-free menu. Yeah, it's $165 for seven courses, but I know how much behind-the-scenes work goes into shaping that experience. So, in my opinion, it's worth it.

Dishes are served in elegant proportions, so you needn't be scared off by the number of courses (but you won't leave craving a dirty burger afterward either). Tasting menus move with the seasons, so in springtime, you might get a stinging nettle agnolotti or a salad accented with sweet pea tendrils and asparagus.

If you prefer to choose your own dishes—or if you want something a little more casual—I find that the restaurant's lunch and dinner menus are pleasingly affordable. There's always a creative selection of housemade pastas, pizzas, and vegetable dishes available, as well as some novel reinterpretations of traditional meat dishes (like the Impossible cigars, which are based on the Moroccan finger food that typically features spiced ground beef rolled tightly in pastry and fried like a thin spring roll).

BURGERLORDS

VEGAN

→ **943 N BROADWAY #102**
   LOS ANGELES, CA 90012

→ **110 N AVENUE 56**
   LOS ANGELES, CA 90042

What's interesting about Burgerlords is that it wasn't always vegan. They made the switch to an all-plant menu in 2020, when owner Frederick Guerrero—who had been considering the abolition of meat for a while—decided that, screw it, it's time. COVID was good for giving people a little nudge on decisions like this.

In an act of vegan burger defiance, they've bypassed the Beyond and Impossible patties and created their own in-house blend, bolstered by vegetables. In fact, these nutrient discs are comprised of around 30 good-for-you ingredients, including barley, shiitake, eggplant, carrots, celery, leeks, red bell peppers, cashews, almonds, and chickpeas. No mention of refined soy protein isolate.

Almost everything is made in-house here, from the sauces to the shakes (which, incidentally, are thickened with a generous scoop of tahini). If you're looking for a nut-free alternative to the garden patties, a tofu version comes crispy and breaded and stuffed into a sandwich along with ranch dressing and slaw, or in nugget form served with spicy dipping sauce. Or fill up on sauce-slathered, salt-brined fries. What I'm saying is you've got options, and almost none of them are highly processed.

I mean, it's what a restaurant should be: real food, carefully prepared, without cutting corners. Burgerlords is proof that fast food can get it right.

MONTY'S GOOD BURGER

VEGAN

→ **FOR LOCATIONS, VISIT MONTYSGOODBURGER.COM**

You've surely heard of Coachella, the weekend-long desert escape that's become one of the most infamous festivals in the world. Now, imagine if Coachella were a burger, free from the confines of animal proteins, unethical practices, and all of the other bad stuff, setting the tone of a party vibe. That's a good burger.

Actually, it would be Monty's Good Burger, which was founded by the same people responsible for the iconic music event itself. When I learned that fact, everything suddenly fell into place. These are seasoned entrepreneurs we're talking about, with great branding and a super smart fast-food concept.

Their strategy was similar to the one taken by Impossible, the makers of the meat-free, "bleeding" burger patty that's featured on the menu. That is, to ignore the vegan audience because, hey, they're not the ones who need help here, and instead market themselves to open-minded omnivores. The Monty's team focused on creating familiarity around the fast-food experience, right down to the sound of sizzling patties smashed onto the grill, which coaxes everyday people through the door.

One of the greatest obstacles for businesses in the plant-based economy is getting people to simply taste the product. Monty's achieves that by simply making delicious burgers that people want to eat. The fact that it's vegan is a bonus—maybe even a surprise—and it often leads diners to realize that vegan food can taste pretty good. Maybe there are other meat-free meals they'd like to try, and so on. It's like a gateway drug to greener, more ethical pastures.

The burger menu is straightforward. There are two styles available: one with cheese and one without, and they're available with single or double patties. To flesh out your meal, add fries, tots (there are, like, ten varieties to choose from, so go nuts), or even a kale Caesar salad. But seriously, if you order a kale salad at a burger joint, you're a psychopath. Authorities have been alerted.

Through their partnership with Impossible, it's estimated that one Monty's burger saves the equivalent of 75 sq ft of land, ½ tub of bathwater, and 18 miles of air emissions (compared to the traditional meat variety). Just another reason why you can feel good about your fast-food choices.

5 MINUTES WITH

BILL FOLD
COFOUNDER OF MONTY'S GOOD BURGER

→ **Where did you get the name?**

Monty is my dog. He is a schnoodle rescue that I found in Riverside. There's a great photo of him on the website.

→ **Let's talk ingredients. What goes into a perfect Monty's burger?**

We use Impossible meat. We buy the ground burger in bulk, and we press our own burger patties from it. We use Follow Your Heart cheese and make all our house sauces with their Vegenaise. From there, it's fresh lettuce, tomatoes, and our pickles, which are actually more like a lightly brined cucumber.

Of course, one of the biggest components of the burger is the bun. We get ours delivered fresh each day from a local bakery in LA called Hearth.

→ **The plant-based dining scene has changed significantly over the past few years. What's your take on the change?**

Companies like Beyond and Impossible have technically followed the design of Gardein and Follow Your Heart, brands that have been around for 20 and 50 years, respectively. But those brands never truly tried to get the taste, look, feel, or texture of meat/dairy products. So when Impossible and Beyond unveiled these products, everything changed dramatically.

Now you have people who are not even vegan or vegetarian who are enjoying plant-based foods, and that just wasn't the case before. You can see it in the very commercialized spread of these products in places like Burger King, Carl's Jr, McDonald's, and KFC. It's much more accessible now, especially in LA and Southern California as a whole. It's not like 15 to 20 years ago when you had to go to Huntington Beach to find this one spot that had really good vegan food. I hope these products have helped win some people over to try some kind of diets like this.

PURA VITA

VEGAN

→ 8274 SANTA MONICA BOULEVARD
(PURA VITA PIZZERIA NEXT DOOR)
WEST HOLLYWOOD, CA 90046

→ 320 S CATALINA AVENUE
REDONDO BEACH, CA 90277

My childhood memories of Italian food all revolve around visits to the local Italian deli. I'd watch family matriarchs lift enormous vats of fresh ricotta into their shopping carts and fuss over cases of tomatoes that would later be crushed, cooked down into pasta sauce, and bottled over the course of a weekend-long family production. And I distinctly remember being frightened of the gruff nonna stationed at the cold meat counter, her eyes thinned and brows furrowed in deep concentration as she shaved near-translucent slices of mortadella with the skill of a medical examiner conducting an autopsy.

As I walk those far, dusty corridors of my memory, I cannot locate a visit that didn't involve meat; oily, vinegary pickled octopus; or excessive amounts of cheese. The pungent smell would hit you like a salted cod on a hot day and stick with you hours after leaving.

So, when I moved to West Hollywood and discovered Pura Vita—the first vegan eatery in the city to buck the burger trend and specialize in Italian food—I was intrigued. Apart from tomatoes, basil, and eggplant, how would they represent this cuisine authentically without the stinky cheeses and meats? Quite easily, evidently.

Let's start with the polpettine: bite-sized meatballs made from mushroom and lentils and served with marinara, macadamia parmigiano, and peppas (meaning, peppers), which are sweet and zingy and punctuated with raisins and pepitas. You could make a meal from the starters and sides alone, but we haven't even ventured into pasta territory yet. Pomodoro, puttanesca—these dishes remind me that quality produce is, at the core, what good Italian food is all about. The showstopper at Pura Vita, however, is the Black Magic Lasagna, a neat square stack of cashew ricotta, béchamel, spinach, mushroom, black truffle cream, and pesto.

Pura Vita puts the tone of WeHo on pause for a moment. It's like a caring friend who pulls you off the dance floor and coaxes you to a quick snack before you thrust yourself back into the general warehouse party that is Santa Monica Boulevard.

→ **What inspired you to open Pura Vita?**

I became vegetarian when I was 10 years old, and by the time I was 12, I was basically vegan. But I grew up in an Italian family in New York, and when I sat my parents down to tell them that I didn't want to participate in eating meat anymore, they didn't really know what to do or how to support me.

My parents are both cooks, and my grandparents were both cooks. So they'd have me in the kitchen with them, watching what they were making, how they were doing it, and letting me tell them what I did want to eat and what I didn't. Being in the kitchen just turned into something I really enjoyed doing. That's how I started learning to cook.

When I was 12, I told my father I was going to open a vegan Italian restaurant. That was a really long time ago. I don't want to give away my age, but it was a long time ago. He laughed at me. I mean, he said, "Yes, of course, honey; you can do anything if you put your mind to it," but he definitely laughed at me.

It took a lot of time to learn about the business side of things and get myself confident enough to take the risk. But opening a vegan Italian restaurant was the plan all along.

→ When did you finally get to open your dream restaurant?

We opened in September of 2018. Then, we opened Pura Vita Pizzeria right next door to the restaurant in May 2020, during COVID. More recently, we opened Pura Vita Redondo Beach—again, during COVID—which is kind of a combination between the restaurant and the pizzeria, but with a full bar and craft cocktail program.

It's right across the street from the beach. It's incredible, more than I ever imagined we could make a reality. The last couple of years have been a wild ride. My original restaurant idea was to have a very small, very old-school, New York Italian vibe. But it just turned into a whole ... thing. I still pinch myself because I'm not exactly sure how it became such an amazing thing. The family and the guests we have are just incredible.

→ What are your best-selling dishes?

Definitely the carbonara pasta—that's our best-selling dish for sure. Then we have a grilled ciabatta with baked ricotta, very simple, which is also very popular. And a lentil mushroom polpettine, which is my version of my mom's meatballs. We don't do a lot of fake meat, but that was one I had to include.

For pizza, we have one that's called Diavolina. It's a sweet and spicy pizza, incredible, probably the best-selling pizza on the menu.

→ What do your staff like to eat there?

They eat everything. Everyone gets staff discounts and meals. I encourage everyone to eat when they're on shift, but most of the front-of-house staff eats with their partners or family. We're all very close, and everyone genuinely enjoys being in the restaurant, being part of what we've built. So they're always here eating.

I know some restaurants tell their staff not to take up a table or a seat at the bar, but I encourage it. I think it's really important for everyone to feel like they're equally and importantly part of something. And it's a great way to fall in love with what we're all creating.

NIC'S ON BEVERLY

VEGAN

→ **8265 BEVERLY BOULEVARD
LOS ANGELES, CA 90048**

I don't know how much more quintessentially LA this restaurant could be. The place is constantly hosting celebrities and Instagram influencers who try to look like celebrities. I think it's largely due to the design of the venue, which is open and airy and features a tropical, fern-fringed outdoor patio that serves as the perfect social media backdrop. You'd actually be committing a crime to your social clout if you didn't take a selfie while holding something fruity and alcoholic here.

So it's a popular venue is what I'm saying.

The "Nic" of the venue's name is none other than Nic Adler himself, the man behind Monty's Good Burger and the culinary program at Coachella. He's got a serious knack for creating food that crosses the omni-vegan brain barrier, enticing those who wouldn't normally think to eat vegan. But therein lies the magic: you don't have to think. Nothing about the place is pushy or preachy or green-washed. The food just looks colorful, fresh, and fun.

Wood-fired, Detroit-style pizza is a menu mainstay. If you don't go for faux meaty options, like pepperoni and BBQ chicken, try the veggie-based pies—especially the Bianco, which is topped with melted leeks, roasted mushrooms, chives, and black truffle vinaigrette. But it's brunch that's the true flex; Just Egg omelets come stuffed with peas and king trumpet mushrooms or triple cheese. As a breakfast sandwich, they're united with crispy potato cakes, American cheese, sausage, and red fresno aioli. With dishes ranging from $15 to $31, it's not exactly everyday morning fuel ... unless you're the Beverly Hills type or Paris Hilton, which you might be. It's LA, after all.

CENA VEGAN

VEGAN

→ **ORDER ONLINE AT CENAVEGAN.COM. PICKUP LOCATION 242 N AVENUE 25 LOS ANGELES, CA 90031**

At this point in time, Cena Vegan is an intangible restaurant. There's no dining room, no servers, and no wine program. But there's an LA pick-up point and an online menu that's stacked with street food favorites, including the obligatory nacho/taco/burrito trinity and plant-based meat sold by the pound.

It was the meat that I discovered first. They're sold under the brand Plant Ranch, which is owned by husband and wife team Carmen Santillan and Mike Simms, along with Mike's high school friend Gary Huerta. Initially planning to set up a food manufacturing business together, the three founders pooled their collective savings—which amounted to $7500—and began producing vegan versions of carne asada, al pastor, and pollo asado. But as their business grew, so did their mission to feed people animal-free alternatives, which ultimately led the team to create a second business: Cena Vegan.

While popular companies, like Beyond, Daring, and Nuggs, have the typical American palate covered for burgers and nuggets, Cena aims to bring Latin American flavors to the table, every table, not just the ones found in mid-century modern dining rooms or an episode of *Selling Sunset*.

DOUBLE ZERO

VEGAN

→ **1700 LINCOLN BOULEVARD**
VENICE BEACH, CA 90291

These are some freaking sexy pizzas. Curvy, crisp, a little char from the wood-burning brick oven, toppings tossed on top—sparingly, delicately, just so.

Yes.

From the mind of Matthew Kenney, this vegan pizza shop in Venice Beach would make anyone weak at the knees, omnis included.

Leading with the pepperoni pie, you'll get a blend of tomato, vegan Calabrian chili, cashew mozzarella, and agave. Heaven. But I love a creamy white sauce on my pizza base, so the Bianca is where I turn next, which boasts cashew mozzarella, macadamia ricotta, pepperoncini, and plant yolk.

But then, I'm hit with the ultimate win: the truffle. No lie, put truffle on literally anything and it will be delicious. Consider this pizza, with cashew cream, wild mushrooms, Tuscan kale, and lemon vinaigrette, evidence of that.

Just in case you're a psycho who doesn't like pizza, there's other stuff for you to order. Double Zero also offers fried artichokes, a bomb cacio e pepe, and salads if you want something more lightweight. But why don't you like pizza? What deep-seated trauma are you refusing to acknowledge?

Double Zero pizzas are available on every functional delivery app in existence, it seems. So, if you prefer to enjoy your pies at home while watching an episode of *The Bold Type*, you're in luck. Just saying, if that's what you'd like to do, you wouldn't be the only one.

How many pizzas can I consume in one sitting, you ask? Oh, I don't know. I like to take a nibble, but you know ... I don't want to reverse all that good work I did today on Peloton.

Four. The answer is four.

5 MINUTES WITH

CARMEN SANTILLAN

COFOUNDER OF CENA VEGAN AND PLANT RANCH

"We never planned for Cena Vegan to be a restaurant or to be serving food to people this long. We started the company because we wanted to be a plant-based meats (PBM) manufacturer.

"We put our money together, got a little taco cart, and set up on York Boulevard, where people could try our Plant Ranch products while we worked to get it into stores and learn about distribution and manufacturing and all that stuff. But the Cena Vegan concept really took off. It was popular almost from day one, exploding into its own business.

"We are still a PBM manufacturer. But we quickly realized we couldn't shut down Cena Vegan. It's just not possible. It feeds a lot of people, and it does a lot of things for the community. My family works at Cena Vegan. It's a family business, and they'd be out of a job if we closed.

"So, we said, 'OK, we didn't set out to do this, but here we are, and we love it.' We love what Cena Vegan has become and what it does, so it needs a permanent home. We intend to set up a brick-and-mortar location in future.

"We're one of the original vendors to start working with Support and Feed. They accept private donations from restaurants and redistribute food to those in need. On a weekly basis, we're producing hundreds of meals to give away.

"At first, we were feeding first responders. Then, we began focusing on the underserved, women's shelters, schools, and communities suffering from food insecurity. We've been doing this sort of community support since day one. It's part of what we do.

"I grew up in Mexico, where, in the smaller towns, people are very poor. They don't have opportunities, so unless you're a college grad or professional, it's very hard to make a living. But entrepreneurship is really strong in the Mexican culture. You see people selling oranges on the side of the street. They're not asking for money; they're actively trying to make a living.

"Where I'm from in Guadalajara, the housewives would set up a table in the front yard or in their living room. They'd hang a lightbulb so people in the neighborhood would know they were cooking dinner. If their specialty was pozole, that's what they would make. They would sell it and try to bring extra money in to support their family. The food would always be delicious because it's a home-cooked meal, it's their signature dish, and it's what they're known for among family and friends.

"It's one of the things I miss so much about Mexico. When we were starting up Cena and Plant Ranch, we wanted to produce a product that would serve the community with a healthy, authentic alternative. We figured that giving was going to be part of the business, always. It's a culture that all the employees know and understand.

"When we're serving tacos on the street, the employees know that they can give a meal to anyone who needs it. If a homeless person walks by or someone who looks like they can't afford a meal, they don't think about it twice. 'Would you like a taco or something to eat?' They feel a responsibility to reach out and give food. Other companies want their employees to ask permission for that, but not with us. It's always been that way."

SAGE PLANT BASED BISTRO (*see* p. 138)

BURGERLORDS *(see* p. 145)

CENA VEGAN *(see* p. 154)

I was surprised to find that the number of vegan restaurants in Miami is relatively small—at least compared to other major cities. But the options are getting better, and for what Miami lacks in dedicated plant-based hospitality, it makes up for with juice bars.

You'll be spoiled for choice in Miami if greased-up beach bros with glistening pecs are your thing. Delete your Tinder profile; it's no longer required. There are 35 miles of beachfront in this city, so it's going to require time, focus, and a Brazilian wax to explore.

If you have the pleasure of traveling with your dog, there are plenty of parks and dog-friendly beaches to keep them entertained as well. Check out Hobie Island Beach Park, the Bark Beach at North Beach Oceanside Park, and South Pointe Park.

Word of warning, though: if you're not a student, don't come here during mid- to late March (aka spring break season). The place transforms into a hellstorm of underaged drinking; one-night encounters; and sweaty, crowded streets. Or maybe I just sold you on it. I really should consider becoming a travel agent.

PLANTA

VEGAN

→ **850 COMMERCE STREET
MIAMI BEACH, FL 33139**

→ **FOR MORE LOCATIONS AND HOME DELIVERY,
VISIT PLANTARESTAURANTS.COM.**

A few years back, hospitality lord Steven Salm watched a little indie flick called *Cowspiracy* and was quickly compelled to go plant-based. The problem was his restaurants weren't built to accommodate this new eating habit.

In true entrepreneurial spirit, Steve decided to solve his problem with another business, a fully plant-based restaurant concept. Teaming up with Chef David Lee, they opened the first Planta location in Toronto. Since then, the group has expanded to seven locations, including two in Miami.

All of the Planta restaurants are known for their beautiful interior decor, but the South Beach location is a shining example of the group's aesthetic: pale wood and cream finishes, the warm glow of dim hanging lights, pops of patterned tiling, and a halo of greenery from indoor ferns. It's no surprise that these restaurants have become celebrity hotspots (and excellent settings for a social media flex).

Glamour aside, the real draw here is clean, produce-driven food. You're not going to find any stodgy seitan or mock meats laden with additives here; everything is built around fresh, sustainable, and ethically sourced ingredients, with a dash of genuine culinary creativity.

I'm an admittedly harsh critic when it comes to vegan restaurant menus, but I'll bet that anyone would appreciate the Planta bianca pizza, whatever their dietary preclusion may be. It's served piping hot with roasted rosemary potatoes, kale, olives, capers, hot chili oil, cashew mozzarella, and onions. The sushi, which arrives hand-rolled with ingredients like ahi watermelon "tuna," heart of palm, and avocado, also gets my vote.

Certain items, including birthday cakes, dumplings, pizzas, and burger patties, can also be ordered online via the Planta at Home service, which ships nationwide.

MINTY Z

VEGAN | WOMAN-OWNED

→ **3206 GRAND AVENUE
MIAMI, FL 33133**

Minty Z's Asian dim sum house was founded by husband and
wife team Alex Falco and Huimin Zhu from the depths of their
house during the 2020 lockdown. That's what I like to see: sheer
entrepreneurial spirit overcoming a crummy situation. I, too,
was stuck inside with my husband during the pandemic,
and like the Minty Z duo, we felt this was an ideal time to build
a business empire.

It's surprising that there aren't more Asian vegan restaurants
around town. The cuisine typically lends itself to an animal-free
diet; there's something about its fresh, bold, and spicy flavors
that's deeply satisfying, even in dishes that don't contain meat
or seafood. Minty Z's take on the category is expressed through
a menu of small tasting plates, noodle and rice bowls, and dim
sum, the latter being the highlight of the show.

Baos, dumplings, rolls, potstickers, and gyoza arrive steaming
from the kitchen, all bursting with plant-forward fillings, like
avocado, cilantro, garlic, and shrooms. Some dishes leverage
modern meat replacements in lieu of traditional proteins, such
as vegan shrimp and Tindle chicken, but Chef Falco tends to focus
more on vegetables seasoned to highlight their unique flavors and
textures with every bite. The carrot and black sesame bao, Cuban
corn wontons, and BBQ jackfruit lo mai gai are particular standouts.
And like any good Asian eatery, the sauce station doesn't disappoint;
all dim sum are served with a house-made ginger-tamari dipping
sauce as well as a dragon concoction (combining chili, peanut, and
vinegar). Can't do gluten? No problem; they've
got you covered with rice-based menu options too.

If you struggle with choice, my recommendation is to skip the
hard decisions and ask for either of the omakase tastings. You can
choose either six courses ($45 per person) or 10 courses ($78 per
person), and all you need to know is that you'll leave happy. Sugar
fiends can round out their meal with chocolate ganache dumplings,
matcha creme brulee, or, my favorite, the bao beignets, which
are deep fried, dusted with five-spice, and served with black
sesame caramel.

EVENTS TO CHECK OUT

TIME OUT MARKET MIAMI

The Time Out Market is a food hall that's been syndicated throughout major cities like New York, Los Angeles, and Melbourne. The Miami pop-up follows a similar format, offering 18 eateries spread across 17,500 square feet. There are always plant-based options available—perhaps more so in recent years, as demand for animal-free alternatives has grown.

Recent vendors have included The Rogue Panda (Chinese), Pho Mo (Vietnamese), Pizzella (Italian), and Clyde's Caribbean, which all provide a multicultural cross-section of Miami's vegetarian and vegan food scenes.

**1601 DREXEL AVENUE
MIAMI, FL 33139**

SEED FOOD & WINE WEEK

The phrase "conscious living festival" makes me think of crystals, aura healing, irritating wind chimes, and a place I generally don't want to go to. But when it's in the context of Seed Food and Wine Week, held annually in Miami, I'm down for it. This is largely because the event offers unlimited food tastings and wine pours, and to be honest, nothing screams the good life to a millennial woman such as myself like an Instagrammable food opportunity and an open bar.

The week-long festival program is packed with celebrity chefs, tastings, cooking demos, and special dining events, and everything is centered around plant-based cuisine. If you can't decide on which event to attend, head to Festival Day and get a taste of everything.

**REGATTA PARK
3500 PAN AMERICAN DRIVE
MIAMI, FL 33131**

BUNNIE CAKES

VEGAN | WOMAN-OWNED

→ **8450 NW 53RD STREET, SUITE H101 DORAL, FL 33166**

Apparently, mom of five and local hero Mariana didn't have enough on her plate raising a small tribe. So when she struggled to find a vegan birthday cake for her two-year-old's upcoming celebration, she decided to take things into her own hands and open up a goddamn bakery. I mean, sometimes if you want something done right, you've got to do it yourself.

At Bunnie Cakes, Mariana is ticking all of the boxes for an inclusive, baked-good experience. Her creations are not only free from animal products, they also omit common allergens, like nuts, soy, and gluten.

Visiting the shop is a celebration in itself. It's as playful as a children's birthday party, only without the weird clown that nobody actually hired nor invited. Barbie-pink walls, heart-lined floors, and lots of sparkles suggest that the parents are having just as much fun in this happy place. The display cases are lined with a wonderland of sweet treats, including guava cupcakes, passion fruit pies, and key lime cakes for those feeling the tropical vibe; mounds of donuts; or classic crowd pleasers, like chocolate, vanilla, cookies-no-cream, and red velvet cakes. Special occasion cakes can be ordered ahead of time with customizable flavors, frosting, and decoration.

Even if you're not in the mood for dessert, visiting Bunnie Cakes will bring you joy. Prepare to be bombarded with cuteness.

YORK
YORK
YORK
YORK
YORK

Everything about New York excites me. I love big cities and the fact that you can spend literal years somewhere and still have no freaking clue what's going on. There's just more of everything. More people. More noises. More smells. More places to go, opportunities to take advantage of, more energy to expend. In fact, when we first visited New York, I announced to my husband Shaun that I never wanted to return to Melbourne again; it was dead to me. It felt like a tiny, insignificant fleck of a city in comparison to New York's electric intensity.

But then, I bought some food at a nearby grocery store.

"We need to fly home immediately," I said to Shaun. "I can't eat anything in this city." Everything tasted like sugar and salt and stale grease, and I pleaded to Shaun that if we didn't go back to Melbourne right away, I could die from malnutrition.

In hindsight, it was an unfair judgment. New York didn't have terrible food; it just had a lot of food, and I had the misfortune of sampling the worst of it, sourced from a crummy, dim-lit bodega in Manhattan. Everything that was convenient and affordable for me to purchase within walking distance seemed to be processed to oblivion, overly packaged, and frighteningly full of additives and flavor enhancers. As someone who's "flexitarian," I found myself eating less meat, seafood, and eggs as a result, purely because what I could buy at the grocery store didn't taste (or look) natural. So, by default, I began filling my cart with plant-based proteins instead. And to this day, I prefer the taste and texture of a Beyond Brat to a Johnsonville pork sausage or the pull of Daring chicken over the disturbingly sized breast of the real deal.

My point, however, is that amazing food did exist in New York. I just had to filter through a bit more crap to find it. Some of those venues are highlighted in this chapter, but not all because you could continue to explore the city for years and still only scratch its surface. Even one of the world's most legendary fine-dining restaurants, **Eleven Madison Park**, made headlines in 2021 with its sudden transition to a plant-based menu—a bold move for such an institution and indicative of what's to come for the future of food.

Other than food, I'm not going to give you any other tips about New York. You don't need them. Just pull up Google Maps, get out on the street, and start walking. There's a lot of ground to cover.

ELEVEN MADISON PARK
11 Madison Avenue
New York, NY 10010

NEW YORK

BEYOND SUSHI

VEGAN

→ **FOR LOCATIONS, VISIT
BEYONDSUSHI.COM/LOCATIONS.**

This storefront sushi operation arrived on the NYC scene in 2012, at a time when seafood hand rolls were still every socialite's go-to accessory. Back then, we all thought sushi was synonymous with raw fish, a delicacy enjoyed only by professional paparazzi posers like Lindsay Lohan and Paris Hilton.

However, when Beyond Sushi opened in a tiny New York City–style space with a menu totally devoid of ocean exploitation, these food fashionistas immediately went out of style. Suddenly, people understood that sushi didn't require ingredients shipped daily from the other side of the continent. It didn't even require seafood. In fact, genuine sushi could be high-quality, affordable, and made entirely from plants. Beyond Sushi was proof it could be done.

At face value, the Beyond Sushi menu reads like you'd expect from any casual American-Japanese restaurant. But that's what makes it so impressive; you don't notice that it's all vegan. That's largely attributed to the generous variety of alternative protein options available. In fact, the whole gang is getting a thorough workout here, from salmon-Zalmon to chick'n, Impossible beef, and jackfruit. No matter what your stance is on this new generation of faux fish and meat, I think these products serve a valuable purpose in getting omnis over the line.

For first-time visitors, I'd recommend trying the spicy mang, a hand roll stuffed with mango in lieu of ocean friends. Trying it for the first time, I was struck by its ability to hit the sensory qualities I was looking to satisfy with a sushi roll. There was no sense of forgoing the "real thing." If anything, compared to the sushi I'd seen in the grab-n-go section of my local Duane Reed, it was the real thing.

Pricing here is ... as you'd expect for New York City, so don't even start complaining.

DELICE &
SARRASIN

VEGAN

→ **20 CHRISTOPHER STREET
NEW YORK, NY 10014**

Before we get to the food, I need to acknowledge the fact that this chic little restaurant is run by a ridiculously good-looking French man and former model named Christophe Caron. I'll give you a moment to Google him. OK, moving on.

Delice & Sarrasin is a tiny venue, but what it lacks in space it makes up for in charm. From the moment you step inside, the hospitality embraces you like a warm hug from Mom, which makes total sense considering Christophe manages the venue alongside his own mom and pop. It's quite a joy to witness the family work together with such clear passion for what they're creating. It's very different from the family-run businesses (and inherent dysfunction) I'm used to seeing on-screen, like in *Succession*, *Arrested Development*, or *Breaking Bad*. Quite different indeed.

While Christophe works front-of-house, mom Yvette handles the hotplates. She used to be a surgeon, so you know she's got that meticulous eye for detail and steady hand required to turn out a perfect galette. Family patriarch Patrick, on the other hand, is a former engineer, so we can be confident that the crepes have sound structure and can withstand the weight of a dense sauce.

Family matters aside, it's the way Delice & Sarrasin uses uncommon ingredients and preparation methods that caught my attention. The sheer novelty of meat and dairy substitutions is part of the attraction; I want to order every dish on the menu, all at once, just to see how they've done it. Brie made from macadamia nuts is a no-brainer, especially knowing how finicky the French are with their cheese. But then, there's salmon shaped from carrot fiber, foie gras formed from tahini, and snails made from oyster mushrooms (which is arguably more appealing than traditional escargot).

They also offer steak tartare made from pea protein, coconut oil, and beets, which immediately had me researching how I could re-create it at home. Their alternate version, made from a mushroom medley, is dense and satisfying. Or for something a little zestier, you can try the crab cakes made from lemon skin and bell peppers. I could marvel at their menu for hours.

Definitely worth a return visit ... or many.

DIRT CANDY

VEGAN | WOMAN-OWNED

→ **86 ALLEN STREET
NEW YORK, NY 10002**

"Vegetables are just candy from the dirt."

That's the opening statement on Dirt Candy's website, and I'm immediately suspicious. This is exactly like when Mom used to tell me that steamed, unsalted broccoli was as delicious as a Papa John's supreme pizza.

But you know what? I love broccoli these days, especially when my husband prepares it. It all comes down to the execution. So with that in mind, I'm going to leave behind logic and get on board with vegetable candy. With Chef Amanda Cohen running the Dirt Candy kitchen, it's a trust fall I'm willing to take.

Amanda made a name for herself as one of the stars of Canada's *Iron Chef*, where she worked only with vegetables, while, and this is only my opinion, the other chefs cheated with animal lard. To me, cooking meat is kind of an easy win. I'm far more excited by chefs who expand their creative scope by exploring plant ingredients in their endless array of colors, shapes, and flavors and utilizing them in new ways.

When Amanda opened Dirt Candy in 2008, it was one of the first high-end restaurants in the city to focus exclusively on vegetables. Menu-wise, we're looking at a single five-course tasting affair for dinner (although an a la carte menu is offered at lunch). The set menu begins with a spectacular spinach mille-feuille to set the tone, which has a flaky puff pastry that provides the scaffolding for layers of vibrant green spinach mousse and smoked pistachio butter. Moving through the menu, things only get better. It's unusual and thoughtful, and the protein isn't missed. By the time the Tower of Terroir course is revealed, it becomes blatantly clear why Cohen likens vegetables to a Payday bar. Imagine a multilevel cake stand displaying beets dressed as lollipops and croutons cast in the shape of Japanese Pocky sticks—only in this instance, with a savory bite.

Dirt Candy is a non-tipping restaurant. So instead of relying on the goodwill of customers, prices are set to reflect the work that goes into running a restaurant of this caliber. I like the idea of paying what the food and service is worth, so I'm all for it.

5 MINUTES WITH

MICHAEL FOX
COFOUNDER AND CEO OF FABLE FOOD CO.

I first met Michael a few years ago when we were both in the very early stages of launching plant-based food startups. Having relocated to the US since then, I was recently thrilled to discover that his company, Fable—which specializes in unbelievably tasty meat alternatives made from shitake mushrooms—had made it to America.

→ **As someone who once wrote a song called "Steak of Glory," you weren't always vegan. Was there a lightbulb moment that made you decide to go plant-based?**

I grew up in Queensland, Australia, which is our equivalent to Texas. I ate a lot of meat and particularly beef as a child! My dad passed away from cancer 15 years ago, and while he was sick, we did a lot of research into healthy diets and realized we should be eating a lot less meat. That kicked off eight years of being a "flexitarian" for me, gradually reducing my meat consumption.

As I read more about the food industry, I became aware of the major ethical and environmental issues with meat consumption. Peter Singer's book *Animal Liberation* was impactful for me, and Jonathan Safran Foer's *Eating Animals* finally tipped me over into going vegetarian seven years ago. I then worked on reducing my dairy and egg consumption, and Michael Greger's book *How Not to Die* and the documentary *Dominion* tipped me over into going fully vegan 18 months ago.

→ **Where can I find Fable?**

Our products are available in Beatnic in NYC/Boston, The Butcher's Daughter in NYC/LA, STK Steakhouses, and Kona Grills across the country. We're rolling out pretty rapidly into restaurants and premium chains in the US, so check out www.fablefood.co for an updated list.

→ **The Fable products are, quite honestly, one of the best meat alternatives I've ever tasted. How are you making that magic happen with mushrooms (and not much else)?**

Mushrooms are more closely related to animals and humans than they are to plants, and we share many similarities. For example, when put in the sun, many mushrooms tan and develop vitamin D just like we do. (You can even do this by putting your store-bought mushrooms in the sun for 10 minutes!) There are also many umami flavor and textural similarities between mushrooms and animals. So we take the mushrooms and leverage these characteristics to make them delicious and meaty, and also make their nutrition more bio-available for our bodies to absorb. My cofounder Jim Fuller is a fine-dining chef, chemical engineer, and mycologist (mushroom scientist), which helps!

→ **As someone who travels a fair bit, do you have any tips on animal-free eating in the US? Any restaurant gems you're willing to share?**

I first went vegetarian back in 2015 while living in LA, and even back then, it was a great place to go plant-based. I loved **The Butcher's Daughter** and Matthew Kenney's Plant Food + Wine on Abbot Kinney. **Veggie Grill** was a regular takeout favorite, and whenever I traveled to New York, I ate at **Beatnic** (called By Chloe back then). There are so many great plant-based options now, and I love that you're sharing so many through this book and helping bring more delicious, healthy, plant-based cheese options to market too!

[I didn't ask him to say that last bit, I swear!]

THE BUTCHER'S DAUGHTER
1205 Abbot Kinney Boulevard
Venice, CA 90291

VEGGIE GRILL
110 S Fairfax Avenue
Los Angeles, CA 90036

BEATNIC
60 W 22nd Street
New York, NY 10010

THE BUTCHER'S DAUGHTER

VEGETARIAN | WOMAN-OWNED

→ **19 KENMARE STREET**
NEW YORK, NY 10012

→ **581 HUDSON STREET**
NEW YORK, NY 10014

→ **271 METROPOLITAN AVENUE**
BROOKLYN, NY 11211

The Butcher's Daughter is where Carrie from *Sex and the City* would hang out if she were boho, vegan, and less occupied with her self-centered thoughts.

Founded by designer and entrepreneur Heather Tierney, The Butcher's Daughter is a chic juice bar and vegetarian restaurant that's underpinned by a down-to-earth philosophy ... but balanced out with a bit of bougie bitch, which is also a requirement of the New York location.

The first location in Nolita opened in 2012, at a time when, sure, there were other vegetarian restaurants dotted around the place, but none that were cool like this one. The restaurant space is breezy, light, and inviting, with a slight Moroccan feel that's expressed through warm tones, a pop of texture, and smart use of communal space. Nothing feels cluttered. It's the kind of venue where one could spend several hours sipping turmeric lattes and working on their plant-based travel guide.

On reviewing the menu, I was struck with a realization: there's a category of cuisine that's missing from the Yelp search filter, and it's called *Sexy Brunch*. An example of what this should look like when performed correctly would be a bit of bubbly met with a tasteful arrangement of burrata antipasto or jackfruit crab cakes, then a tower of rice flour pancakes drooling with coconut and berry compote.

Keep Insta stories on standby for this restaurant because, judging by its polished appearance, it was definitely designed with social media opportunities in mind. I wouldn't be at all surprised if Gwyneth Paltrow shot an episode of *The Goop Lab* here; I can picture her now, emerging from a crochet womb and floating through the entrance to order a wellness smoothie. She'd definitely purchase one of the Eau De Butcher's Daughter room sprays too, which are available on the Shop section of the restaurant's website and are made in collaboration with AYDRY & Co.

LADYBIRD

VEGAN

→ **111 E SEVENTH STREET
NEW YORK, NY 10009**

Speaking of restaurants tailor-made for the Instagram generation, Ladybird tops my list. Strikingly pink walls, plush velvet seating, shiny brass-framed mirrors, hanging greenery, and completely over-the-top bathrooms set the scene for some kind of opulent, millennial Garden of Eden. You'd probably be breaking a bylaw if you didn't take a selfie here and immediately upload it to all social platforms #glamsquad #luxury.

It's clear that Ladybird is the work of pros. It's owned by Ravi DeRossi, who's earned himself some cred in the NYC plant-based dining scene as the man behind the Overthrow Hospitality group (they run an entire fleet of mission-based bars and restaurants, including Amor Y Amargo, Proletariat, Avant Garden, Cadence, and Soda Club). At Ladybird, Ravi's team brings together the two things they do best: booze and vegan bites.

The category is tapas. It's an ideal meal format for socialites who like to appear as though they're eating, but also excellent for people like me, whose idea of a great night out is tasting every dish on the menu then having a nap while my husband drives us home. Tapas enables this dream to become a reality.

At Ladybird, I'd begin with the ricotta toast, a crunchy spear of bread spread thick with vegan ricotta cheese and dressed with marinated white beans and roasted broccolini. Follow quickly with pea fritters and a dish of avocado, wakame, black garlic ponzu, fried garlic chips, and crispy shallots. From there, I'd dive into the Chardonnay and artichoke fondue and probably ask for extra bread so I could mop up every last smear of sauce.

Given that New York is a 24-hour city, don't pass on Ladybird's late-night hours. Their kitchen offers a special menu starting at 11 p.m. on Thursday, Friday, and Saturday nights, so you no longer have an excuse to hit up Mickey D's at midnight for emergency fries.

SCREAMER'S PIZZERIA

VEGAN

→ **620 MANHATTAN AVENUE**
BROOKLYN, NY 11222

→ **685 FRANKLIN AVENUE**
BROOKLYN, NY 11238

There are two types of people in my book: those who watched shows like *Saved by the Bell* and *The Fresh Prince of Bel-Air* on a Saturday morning in the early '90s, and those who are watching the reboots for the first time now. To be fair, the updated versions have a lot more potty language and blatant recognition of the gender/race/class issues that were kept alive by their predecessors, so they have that in their favor. But the old versions had undeniable rad vibes that simply can't be replicated by NBC's youth outreach department.

I'll hand it to Screamer's Pizzeria, though. Their branding has got me all nostalgic and texting my mom to see if she still has my old VHS tapes in the garage. She doesn't. That's OK because I have pizza to remind me of the good times, and Screamer's is selling it by the slice.

There are two locations to choose from—Greenpoint and Crown Heights—and both have different menus, so if you're serious about this pizza quest, plan to visit both. Because I'm a wild gal, I tend to buck tradition and beeline for pies with a creamy white-sauce base as opposed to the tomato variety. They've got a cracker here called the White Pie, which comes topped with garlic oil, ricotta, and oregano, and it's available at both locations. Pizza progressives might also like the Artichoke Pie (hot pesto, cheese, seitan sausage, artichoke hearts, and roasted peppers) or the Reuben, which takes the classic American pizza into Jewish deli territory with the addition of sauerkraut and Thousand Island dressing.

While word on the street is generally very positive, Screamer's does get a bit of social media pushback on the cheese situation (which is not unusual for any business trying to break away from the boundaries of dairy). Some say it's too gummy, doesn't melt well, or smells like beans (which makes sense since some vegan cheeses are made from soybeans or bean starch). But unless you're flying in straight from Naples where you regularly judge the local mozzarella competition, I think you'll enjoy it just fine. Otherwise, go for the pies made with almond ricotta. Or take full advantage of the build-your-own option and leave cheese out of it.

KAJITSU

VEGETARIAN

→ **125 E 39TH STREET, FOURTH FLOOR
NEW YORK, NY 10016**

Kajitsu means "fine day" or "day of celebration" in Japanese. To me, any eating occasion is a good reason to celebrate and pop open a few cans of Ghia Le Spritz (seriously, if you haven't tried these nonalcoholic apéritifs yet, they're divine).

Shojin cuisine is a style of cooking that originates from Zen Buddhism—a spiritual practice that condemns the killing of animals—and relies heavily on plant ingredients, like soy and konjac. Flavors are delicate and largely aided by soy sauce, dashi (a stock made from kelp), and fermentation methods as opposed to salt or other additives. Onion and garlic are typically avoided, as are any overpowering seasonings. Without these, the true flavors of each ingredient in the dish can be appreciated.

Japanese cuisine has always been known for its thoughtfulness, precision, and intent, and that attention to detail has earnt Kajitsu a coveted Michelin star. There's only one menu option available: the 10-course omakase ($120), which is a succession of perfectly prepared bites and bowls chosen by the chef. The menu changes monthly, but previous dishes have included kuchidori (housemade sesame tofu seasoned with wasabi and served in a crispy rice wafer) and oshinogi (a vegetable jelly wrapped in fresh bamboo). To fully immerse yourself in the omakase experience, consider the tea and sake pairing, which is designed to complement each course.

This thoughtful approach doesn't stop at food. Even the servingware is reflective of Shojin philosophy; some of the ceramics sourced by the restaurant are more than 200 years old, having been carefully maintained and repaired out of deep respect for the master Japanese potters who created them.

Note: Kajitsu is located on the fourth floor of the building and doesn't have an elevator (so it's not wheelchair accessible).

SOL SIPS

VEGAN

→ **276 KNICKERBOCKER AVENUE BROOKLYN NY 11237**

How's this for small-business inspiration: Francesca Chaney opened Sol Sips as a college student when she was just 22 years old. Total boss. Not only that, she managed to build a restaurant that's genuinely affordable and caters to those who need access to healthy food regardless of their ability to pay.

Considering Brooklyn's history of gentrification (now evident through an abundance of single-origin coffee options, high AF avocado prices, and impossible rents), Sol Sips is a refreshing disruption to its Bushwick neighborhood. Here's the setup: meals are offered on a sliding payment scale, which depends on what patrons can afford. EBT/SNAP cardholders can sign up for free meal vouchers, but if you're ordering one of the restaurant's local meal delivery kits, you can self-select the level of payment you can afford (either $60, $80, or $90). It's a fine example of a social enterprise that's truly getting involved and improving the community's access to nutritious, cruelty-free food.

So, what's on the menu? Regulars like the bacon, egg, and cheese sandwich, which comes loaded with scrambled chickpea eggs, vegan cheese, tempeh bacon, and tomatoes on a chia seed bun. The mac and cheese is another familiar entry point and provides a soft introduction for those who are still cautious about vegan food. For the already initiated, the ripe plantains (stuffed with stew beans, peppers, onions, and cheese) and the crispy fried okra both scored highly on my flavor test. And don't forget the bevs, as there's a solid selection of colorful, antioxidant-packed smoothies available to round out your meal.

CARAVAN OF DREAMS

VEGAN

→ **405 E SIXTH STREET**
NEW YORK, NY 10009

In 1991, Spanish founder Angel Moreno built Caravan of Dreams with his bare hands. This is not an exaggeration; he physically built this restaurant himself with bricks and wooden beams. Since then, it's become a pillar of the East Village vegetarian and vegan community—a place to eat, educate, and create.

If your parents were a little left-leaning or if you immediately recognize the terms "macrobiotic" and "ashtanga yoga," you'll know exactly what I mean when I say the menu is "old-school vegetarian." I'm talking brown rice, tempeh, grilled tofu, and a ton of raw vegetables. There's still a market for it; not everyone wants to dust themselves in modified starch or ram processed Lightlife hot dogs into their face. This is what's truly meant by "clean eating."

Raw food enthusiasts will be in absolute heaven at Caravan of Dreams. A cucumber manicotti (cucumber pasta stuffed with cashew cheese, avocado, arugula, mushroom, and nutmeat) is a totally unfaithful rendition of the Italian classic, and there's no need to apologize for that. It delivers the flavor. As does a serving of raw nori rolls stuffed with walnut pâté, avocado, apples, jicama, sprouts, radish, and sauerkraut. If you're not used to eating this kind of (fresh) food, then sure, you might find it bland. But if that's the case, I'd argue that a raw detox is probably just what you need.

Orlando is a family-friendly travel destination, largely due to its disproportionate number of theme parks. I've counted four **Walt Disney World** megaverses (Magic Kingdom, Animal Kingdom, Epcot, and Hollywood Studios), three owned by **Universal** (Universal Studios, Islands of Adventure, and Epic Universe), SeaWorld, Discovery Cove, **LEGOLand**, and Busch Gardens. I will note that some of these parks are deeply troubling for anyone concerned about animal welfare, so if seeing animals in captivity or forced to perform all day makes your heart cry, I'd stick with the roller coasters and LEGOs.

Heading to Disney's magical arena? You're going to need a roadmap of all the plant-based dining options available. The park's website is quite helpful for this and points out where to find everything, from animal-free bratwurst and burgers on the boardwalk to dumplings, desserts, popcorn, pretzels, and their infamous pineapple Dole whip (just be sure to order a fruit flavor and not vanilla, as the latter contains dairy). I will, however, warn that whatever your dining preference, you'll burn cash at a rapid rate if you intend to buy all your meals on-site. So pack as many snacks as you can comfortably carry.

If disturbingly chirpy Disney employees dressed in mouse costumes are not your thing, try the **Kennedy Space Center Visitor Complex**. Nerd-level unlocked. It's not unheard of to witness a live rocket launch during a casual visit. For something more laid-back, there are the pristine dunes of **Clearwater Beach**, where you'll find street performers, dolphins, sea turtles, and a bunch of hot buns in Brazilian-cut bathing suits or sporting massive wedgies.

ORLANDO

**WALT DISNEY
WORLD ORLANDO**
disneyworld.disney.go.com

UNIVERSAL ORLANDO
universalorlando.com/web/en/us

LEGOLAND
legoland.com/florida

**KENNEDY SPACE CENTER
VISITOR COMPLEX**
Space Commerce Way
Merritt Island,
FL 32953

THE GREENERY CREAMERY

VEGAN OPTIONS AVAILABLE

→ **420 E CHURCH STREET #112**
   ORLANDO, FL 32801

→ **HENRY'S DEPOT**
   212 W FIRST STREET
   SANFORD, FL 32771

You might think you know ice cream, but until you've experienced it freshly made from a small batch using entirely natural ingredients (don't get me started on that bulk crap you'll find at the grocery store), you know nothing. Absolutely nothing!

The Greenery Creamery is here to show you a better sweet life. The dessert parlor serves a spectacular range of animal-free ice creams, handmade from ingredients like coconut, peanut butter, sunflower butter, almond, and soy.

You can preorder an entire vegan ice cream cake (I strongly suggest the Speculoos cookie butter flavor), or stop by for a solo scoop. There's also vegan cake classes available on Saturday mornings, which cost a pretty reasonable $60 per person or $65 per couple (including one glorious cake).

In addition to plant-based desserts, the Greenery Creamery offers organic dairy-based ice creams to keep the boomers happy. Get one for your uncle Jeff to shut him up when he starts talking about how climate change is a conspiracy.

DHARMA SOUTHERN KITCHEN

VEGAN

→ **MARKET ON SOUTH**
2603 E SOUTH STREET
ORLANDO, FL 32803

Chef-owner Shaun Noonan took the long route to the land of fine vittles. A self-declared punk kid and general troublemaker, he did what many men with arm sleeve tattoos inevitably must do as a rite of passage: he became a chef.

Shaun quickly found himself immersed in Chicago's fine-dining scene, making what I like to call "art food," which is great, but let's be honest, food plated with tweezers doesn't exactly scream comfort. And if you watched Hulu's *The Bear*, you'll know I'm not referring to the food, but the physical and mental comfort of the professionals creating it.

These days, Shaun operates Dharma Southern Kitchen, a place where the people of Orlando can get their fixin's without fancy tablecloths or minor panic attacks when the bill arrives. Southern comfort favorites are reimagined here with plant-based chicken, jackfruit, and fried green tomatoes, and most dishes come oozing with enough creamy slaw and cashew cheese to make diners forget—albeit, momentarily—that they're eating a little greener.

LEGUMINATI

VEGAN

→ **2401 CURRY FORD ROAD
ORLANDO, FL 32806**

Rebecca Larsen, a certified holistic health coach and integrative nutrition graduate, created the Vegan Orlando online directory in 2014 as a way of tracking the city's best animal-free dining digs. I can only assume she was either saddened by a lack of options or completely inspired by those that did exist because a year later she was compelled to open her own food venture called Leguminati.

What started out as a food truck is now permanently hosted by Hourglass Social House, a former gas station converted into a community hub. At the Leguminati stall, patrons are presented with a concise menu of toasted wraps packed full of vegan-friendly yet satisfying ingredients. There's the Cali Crunch made with chick'n, rice paper "bacun," sriracha, guacamole, tomato, and vegan ranch. Or if you like getting your hands dirty, you can try the Sloppy Crunch, which has a vegan beef crumble, bacun, and a "slop sauce" concoction.

Hourglass is a destination in itself, so be sure to check out the other local vendors and breweries while you're there.

VEGGIE GARDEN

VEGETARIAN | VEGAN OPTIONS AVAILABLE

→ **1216 E COLONIAL DRIVE #11**
   ORLANDO, FL 32803

Orlando's "Little Vietnam" dates back to the 1970s, when thousands of refugees fled the Vietnam War and settled in the area. As they established new lives, an industrious community of small businesses began to form, with restaurants playing a significant role in the local economy's growth. These days, the Little Vietnam area is known as the Mills 50 District, a stretch of streets lined with numerous Thai, Chinese, Korean, and Vietnamese eateries. And among them sits a humble vegan gem: Veggie Garden.

Here, Vietnamese noodle soup assumes the position of MVP on the menu. In keeping with tradition, steaming hot bowls of flavorful broth arrive piled high with fresh herbs, bean sprouts, and scallions. All the soups are either vegetarian or vegan, and there's an option to boost protein levels by adding soybean ham or tofu. In my opinion, a nourishing noodle soup is the best way to nurse a hangover and replace essential electrolytes. For others, it's simply a good meal.

Most of the dishes at Veggie Garden are free from animal derivatives, but do note that some of their desserts and drinks contain milk, so be sure to check the menu first (or if in doubt, ask a server).

BLACK BEAN DELI

VEGAN OPTIONS AVAILABLE

→ **1835 E COLONIAL DRIVE
ORLANDO, FL 32803**

Another Mills 50 District destination, Black Bean Deli is a Cuban-inspired, all-day eatery. It's not specifically plant-based, but the range of animal-free options available on the menu made it a worthy contender for inclusion here.

A word of warning first: don't go here if you can't stomach the smell of meat or don't want to support a restaurant that features it so predominantly. Meat is the cornerstone of this style of cuisine, and some may find that overwhelming. But absolutely do come for the vegan empanadas, fried plantains, yuca with cilantro aioli, and yellow rice and black beans—all of which make a delicious and hearty meal without the animal protein. There's also juices, wine, and coffee available (with oat milk available on request).

I know some people refuse to eat anything from a business that also sells meat, but I like seeing businesses that recognize the need to bring plant-based proteins to the forefront and are willing to invest in them. After all, perfect is the enemy of progress.

PHILAD
PHILAD
PHILAD
PHILAD
PHILAD

ELPHIA
ELPHIA
ELPHIA
ELPHIA
ELPHIA

At first glance, Philadelphia seems to be famous for three things, all food-related. There's the cheesesteak, a hot mess of thinly sliced beef and melted American cheese stuffed into a long roll. Then, there's the hoagie, Philly's signature response to the Italian sub or hero sandwich, which is packed full of sliced meats, cheeses, and veggies. And finally, Philadelphia cream cheese, which actually originated in New York and was never manufactured in Philadelphia in the first place.

There are probably other non-food-related things that Philly is famous for, but as someone whose life revolves around procuring and creating lovely things to eat, I don't care about those.

Food tourists should make a visit to **Reading Terminal Market** their first priority on the travel itinerary. Established in 1893, it's one of the oldest public markets in the country, and to this day, it remains a one-stop shop for fresh produce, specialty sweets, flowers, art, and gifts. Aside from the obvious fruit and veg, there's a fair number of food vendors selling vegetarian and vegan fares. Give Carmen's Famous Italian Hoagies and Cheesesteaks a whirl for a seitan-based alternative to the city's staple, or check out Luhv Vegan Deli for a dedicated range of vegan and gluten-free sandwiches.

The market is open until 6 p.m. daily, but vendors tend to sell out early. So don't come running to me if you stay out dancing until 3 a.m., sleep in, and consequently miss out on a great eggplant deal.

I'm not joking about the temptation of dance either. Philadelphia was the first city in the United States to launch a major LGBTQ+ tourism campaign, with the delightful slogan "Get Your History Straight and Your Nightlife Gay®." Its "Gayborhood," which stretches from Pine Street to Chestnut Street and 11th Street to Broad Street, has such a high concentration of nightspots, restaurants, and bars that it almost gives West Hollywood a run for its money. It's not a random marketing grab either; one of the first large-scale LGBTQ rights demonstrations in the United States was held in Philadelphia in 1965, and it was also home to Barbara Gittings, an activist widely recognized for her contribution to the LGBTQ rights movement.

Stepping away from the party pace for just a moment, there's a strong slow-food movement here that provides sanctuary for sustainable foodies, animals, and community members seeking healthy produce. **Greensgrow** urban farm is a nonprofit that aims to supply the public with locally grown food and educate them on sustainable agricultural practices they can re-create in their home gardens and kitchens. Their on-site, Pay-What-You-Can farmstand sells organic produce at a very low cost and without the unnecessary food miles associated with traditional groceries. Everything comes directly from the farm itself or from local growers within a 150-mile radius of Philadelphia.

Visitors to the farm can also spend some quality time with the resident chickens, Ping the duck, or Milkshake, their infamous pet pig.

READING TERMINAL MARKET
1136 Arch Street
Philadelphia, PA 19107

GREENSGROW
2501 E Cumberland Street
Philadelphia, PA 19125

VEDGE

VEGAN

→ **1221 LOCUST STREET**
PHILADELPHIA, PA 19107

As endearing as they are, there's only so many veggie burgers
a human can handle. So let's turn to the finer end of the dining
spectrum, with vegetable-only restaurant Vedge. Founded by
James Beard Award–nominated Chefs Rich Landau and Kate
Jacoby, the restaurant explores the untapped potential of everyday
ingredients, like broccoli, tofu, and carrots, and presents them
in a format that's not only delightfully unexpected but delicious.

   Considered a standout of Philadelphia's vegetarian/vegan dining
scene, Vedge is open for dinner from Tuesday to Saturday, but I'd
strongly suggest getting in when doors open at 5 p.m. for happy
hour. While the drink list is short, it's well considered, and fans of
natural wine will be in a state of ethereal joy among the selection
of skin-contact grapes.

   Dishes here are served as medium "plates," which are a little larger
than traditional tapas but not enough for a meal on their own. Vedge
recommends ordering three per person, but my strategy is to bring
a group so I can order as many plates as possible and work through
the entire menu, bite by bite.

   Flavors will vary by the season, but you might catch the carrot
rillettes (served with pumpernickel, smoked mustard, grilled celery,
cucumber, and dill) or stuffed avocado surrounded by a smear
of almond romesco and piled high with crispy rice and black salt.
Desserts are equally interesting, with an apricot tart—served
with halva frangipane and black sesame brittle—proving to be
a standout.

   Is it expensive? Of course, it's fine dining! But it's reasonable
for the attention to detail you'll receive, both in service and the
quality of the food. That's why the locals keep coming back.

ALL THE WAY LIVE

VEGAN | WOMAN-OWNED

→ **6108 GERMANTOWN AVENUE
PHILADELPHIA, PA 19144**

I have a soft spot for old-school, whole-food recipes. As a teenager, I went through a phase of scouring thrift stores for 1970s and '80s vegetarian cookbooks, all worn and faded, with pages of curious dinner party ideas, most of which seemed to involve a wobbly cucumber jelly as the centerpiece. The animal-free alliance ate differently back then; there was far less reliance on modern meat substitutes, and nobody was talking about "cell lines," "precision fermentation," or growing chicken breast without the bird itself. But they had, like, tomatoes and lentils.

The menu at All the Way Live reminds me of those cookbooks in a really wholesome way. It's primarily based on raw food, vegetables, unrefined grains, and pulses, with a small selection of cooked dishes, such as curries and a lasagna made from zucchini sheets instead of pasta. The burgers, which seem obligatory on any US menu at this point, take a hard pass on manufactured meat substitutes, relying instead on nutmeat, chickpea patties, mushrooms, and jackfruit for some heft between the buns.

There's desserts too, and hear me out before passing judgment on this, but I was extremely excited by their carob cake. I know carob gets a bad rap, and we're all doing dairy-free chocolate now anyway, but I'm not giving up on this treat that became a staple of my childhood. If you had parents who were health freaks, you'll know what I'm talking about. In a pantry stocked with buckwheat, legumes, raw nuts, and long-life soy milk, the odd carob bud would be a mind-blowing thrill. This all went downhill when I was about 10 years old and discovered bubblegum-flavored ice cream and consequently accused my parents of child abuse for hiding these delicious foodstuffs from my face for so long. But in hindsight, they were probably on to something and would have really liked All the Way Live.

HIPCITYVEG

VEGAN | WOMAN-OWNED

→ **127 S 18TH STREET**
PHILADELPHIA, PA 19103

→ **121 S BROAD STREET**
PHILADELPHIA, PA 19107

→ **FOR MORE LOCATIONS,**
VISIT HIPCITYVEG.COM/LOCATIONS.

It's fast food for conscious consumers. The menu is short, featuring a small selection of burgers, sandwiches, salads, and fries, and utilizes ingredients that arrive fresh each day. But the real focus is on sustainability, which extends beyond the plant-based menu through thoughtful packaging and design.

Containers, cups, straws, and utensils are entirely compostable, and the venues themselves are built using salvaged wood, recycled plastic, and energy-efficient lights and appliances.

PROOF THAT HOSPITALITY ENTREPRENEUR NICOLE MARQUIS TOTALLY DOMINATES

Do local governments still award a "key to the city" to esteemed citizens? If so, I'm nominating Nicole Marquis for her service to vegan hospitality in the Greater Philadelphia area. Not only is she the brains behind HipCityVeg, she's also the boss of boozy boudoir/bar Charlie was a sinner and Bar Bombón.

It wouldn't be the first time Nicole has been recognized for her achievements.

She's already been awarded the Hispanic Chamber of Commerce's Hispanic Business of the Year award (2019), the StarChefs Rising Stars award (2019), the Best of Philly award (three times), and the Philadelphia Business Journal's 40 Under 40 award (2017). Sheesh! But as someone who happily admits that their life revolves around food, I'm most impressed by Nicole's contributions to the local food scene.

BAR BOMBÓN

VEGAN | WOMAN-OWNED

→ **133 S 18TH STREET
PHILADELPHIA, PA 19103**

A party of Puerto Rican and plant-based flavors from midday
to midnight (or later). That's the gist of Bar Bombón, a vibrant
Latin-inspired cantina serving clean classics every day of the week.

The tortillas are made in-house, and most of the proteins come
from non-GMO soy and organic grains. Choose from chorizo-spiced
beef, chicken, and smoked tempeh, then add a healthy amount
of black beans and rice to fill out a hearty lunch. You could even
add a margarita or two if work won't interfere with the inevitable
afternoon siesta. Or you can come for weekend brunch, when
there's a solid variety of dinner-for-breakfast dishes, such as Just
Egg tortas, Spanish meatballs, empanadas, and fried plantains.

CHARLIE WAS A SINNER.

VEGAN | WOMAN-OWNED

→ **131 S 13TH STREET
PHILADELPHIA, PA 19107**

Nicole Marquis has been instrumental in putting Philadelphia's vegan dining scene on the map. After opening her first restaurant, a fast-casual burger concept called HipCityVeg, she noticed that the demand for plant-based cuisine had begun to swell. Despite all odds (remember: we're talking about the epicenter of Philly cheesesteaks territory), the locals were embracing meat alternatives at a rapid velocity. At the time, most of that was driven by our cultural acceptance of burgers in any and all formats. As such, Nicole felt there was more to be done.

The city needed a vegan speakeasy.

Not in the literal sense. There was no need for moonshine to be ferried across an underground network of bathtubs and bars by dapper men sporting thin mustaches and flat caps. But there was definitely a white space in the market for a sexy, dim-lit nighttime spot, a prohibition-inspired bar to make the city of Philadelphia complete.

That's how Charlie was a sinner. came to be. Taking its name from a block of 13th Street that was once known as "The Sin Strip," the moody cocktail lounge is all about small plates, strong drinks, and a flourish of theater.

The cocktails are legit. They're thoughtfully put together using only plant-based ingredients and no blasphemous premixes. Take The Metamorphosis as a case in point; it's a zippy, pretty concoction of butterfly pea flower–infused gin, elderflower liqueur, vegan egg white, grapefruit, and lemon. Or for something simple but equally impactful, the Pink Moon melds champagne and vodka together with strawberry, fennel shrub, and lime.

The sinner kitchen is open late, serving snacky morsels that provide a steady buffer against the booze. I'm not talking about a sad dish of bar nuts either; I mean serious menu items, dishes you'd expect to find at brunch on Sunday. Maybe an avo toast or Caesar salad, or a banh mi brimming with spicy grilled tofu, cilantro aioli, and pickled veg. The staff doesn't drive the vegan angle hard either, even though the venue is entirely plant-based. This makes it an ideal location for Bumble dates, when you don't want to announce your veganism in the first sentence (because labels don't define you) but you do want to suggest a place that everyone can enjoy.

CRUST VEGAN BAKERY

VEGAN | WOMAN-OWNED

→ **4409 MAIN STREET**
PHILADELPHIA, PA 19127

Shannon and Meagan met after their friends were absolutely convinced that the two would hit it off. During somewhat of a business blind date, the pair felt inspired to build a bakery together, and that's how Crust was born. Was veganism the common denominator here or simply an alarming obsession with baked sweets? We may never know. But we should all be grateful for this serendipitous meeting of minds because now everyone can enjoy everything from plant-based toaster pastries to buns and brownies, all completely animal-free and made on location in Philly.

This is a proudly woman-owned business that puts just as much time and attention into its products as it does its employees. The Crust team makes a point of supporting and donating to the local community and providing ethical employment opportunities. It's all part of the mission statement, which they summarize perfectly with the line, "We keep it political because food is political." Hell yes!

But onto cakes. There's always a selection of freshly baked creations available in store, but you can also call in an order to guarantee your favorite flavor is available. The Crust crew also offers customizations and wedding cakes if you need something a bit next-level for a special occasion. But be warned: willpower is required when visiting the shop. The sultry sweet temptation of a brownie bar, sugar-frosted cookie, cherry danish, or pistachio-cardamom scone may be too overwhelming to bear. Don't fight it. Just bring extra cash.

CRUST VEGAN BAKERY'S MOLASSES COOKIES

MAKES 22 COOKIES

¾ cup sugar, plus extra for rolling the cookies in

½ cup unsalted Earth Balance butter (or other plant-based butter)

½ cup unsulphured blackstrap molasses

1 Ener-G egg (or equivalent egg replacement)

2 cups flour

2 tsp baking soda

1 tsp cinnamon

½ tsp salt

½ tsp ginger

Preheat the oven to 350°F and line a cookie sheet.

Mix sugar and Earth Balance butter with an electric mixer until smooth and fluffy. Add molasses and Ener-G, and beat for an additional minute.

Add dry ingredients and stir together until a thick dough forms.

Scoop dough into small balls. Roll each ball in the extra sugar, then gently press them onto a lined cookie sheet at least 2 inches apart. Bake for 12 minutes and allow to cool on a wire rack.

These cookies tend to spread a lot during the last few minutes of baking, so be sure to keep enough distance between them to allow for expansion.

PORT
PORT
PORT
PORT
PORT

LAND
LAND
LAND
LAND
LAND
LAND

I've gleaned most of my cultural guidance from the TV series *Portlandia*. It's a bit dated now, but the lessons learned from its mythical portrayal of the city's most painful hipsters will stick with me for life.

In reality, the real Portland is nothing like the show, but there are a few characteristics that ring true: it has a progressive food scene, a proclivity toward artisan products, and a large number of restaurants that cater to vegan and other dietary requests.

In some parts of the world, happy hour seems reserved for students and ladies on the lookout for $1 Champagne specials. But something I love about the US is that happy hours are just part of standard operating procedure. You'll find some good ones in Portland—just aim for the sweet spot of 4 p.m. to 6 p.m.

There's a lot to explore in this city, but before we hop on the food trail, I want to highlight a couple of initial pit stops you should consider. The first is **Food Fight! Grocery**, an ethical grocery store that's plastered with personality and has a genuine mission behind it. Their commitment to animals, the earth, and "non-turd" people are sensibilities we could all live by.

If you're into body art, check out **Scapegoat Tattoo**. It's a vegan tattoo studio that uses animal-free ink, unlike the gritty studio you might find yourself in at 2 a.m. after an innocent night at the local discotheque. Oftentimes, tattoo studios use black ink made from bone char or shellac (beetles). But Scapegoat is having none of it, and they don't use glycerin in the mix (which often contains animal fat) or lanolin (the grease contained in lamb wool) in the tracing paper either.

PORTLAND

FOOD FIGHT! GROCERY
11155 NE Halsey Street
Portland, OR 97220

SCAPEGOAT TATTOO
1233 SE Stark Street
Portland, OR 97214

BLACK WATER BAR

VEGAN

→ **835 NE BROADWAY
PORTLAND, OR 97232**

Black Water Bar serves the kind of food that is entirely appropriate for times when beer, bourbon, and bands take priority. There's a time and place for acai bowls, and this is not it.

On the menu, there are multiple iterations of fried potato. Fries are the standard format, but you can go with the chili cheese variety to spice things up or order the tots if you're feeling cute. They also offer nachos, pierogies, "wingz," and a selection of hefty burgers and sandwiches for those settling in for the long haul. Whatever you choose, it's probably going to get messy, but remember, you're in a live music venue and the tone has already been set.

It's important to keep that in mind as you approach the cocktail menu too. They're not doing elderberry infusions or small-batch mezcal, so don't ask. Instead, consider a Lebowski bulldog (vodka, Kahlua, coconut milk, and cola) or a tangy michelada. The drinks are all priced between $8 and $12, so craft cocktails it is not. A good time, however, it most certainly is.

With indoor dining rules leaving hospitality venues feeling flaky, Black Water Bar has branched out into online delivery. You'll find their entire menu to enjoy at home on all the usual apps (beverages included).

THE SUDRA

VEGAN

→ **906 N FREMONT STREET**
PORTLAND, OR 97227

→ **28 NE 28TH AVENUE**
PORTLAND, OR 97232

→ **4589 SW WATSON AVENUE**
BEAVERTON, OR 97005

It's not traditional Indian food—at least not what comes to mind when we think of Indian food in the Western world, like butter chicken and dahl. But at The Sudra, owner Sanjay Chandrasekaran has created something arguably more interesting, combining his Indian heritage with the experience of growing up in New Mexico. What results is a cacophony of flavors and spices and a welcome departure from the make-at-home Indian curries or jar sauces that many of us are used to.

There's a lot to choose from at The Sudra, so factor in a little extra time to navigate the menu. Bowls of kale and tofu "paneer," lentil kofta, and jackfruit vindaloo come in whole or half servings, while a long list of $5 sides can be added to ensure diners don't miss out on tasting a bit of everything. Alternatively, the Plate comes with a little bit of everything: bites of pickled broccoli and cauliflower pakora, black bean masala, kale in tahini dressing, tamarind chutney, coconut yogurt, radishes, and brown basmati rice.

Chandrasekaran is somewhat of a hospitality legend around these parts, and The Sudra is not his only vegan venue. For more of his culinary hits, check out Rabbits Cafe (for plant-based bowls and smoothies), Daylily Coffee Shop, and the latest addition, Lilla, a vegan handmade pasta shop.

DOE DONUTS

VEGAN | WOMAN-OWNED

→ **4110 NE SANDY BOULEVARD
PORTLAND, OR 97212**

In keeping with Portland's M.O., Doe likes to keep things weird. This artisan donut shop's creations defy logic at times, yet always seem to work no matter how whacky they are. They keep you on your toes with an ever-changing seasonal menu of fried vegan dough puffs, but previous standouts have included the CBD Couch Potato (chocolate glaze, kettle chips, and pretzel truffle), the Mango Sticky Rice (mango glaze, coconut sticky rice, and sesame seeds), and the Portland Fog (organic Earl Grey glaze, fresh whip, and fair trade vanilla bean).

Unlike traditional donut shops, Doe Donuts isn't afraid to dive into savory territory. Anyone familiar with Asian bakeries will understand that this concept is not that radical. I remember one particular encounter in Singapore when I tried a creamy curry donut, and I've been thinking about it fondly ever since. Doe's spin on the savory puffs include a punchy Mexican corn concoction, a bacon mac-and-cheese-filled donut, and a BBQ jackfruit version ; its rich, meaty texture offsets the sugar rush of the eight glazed and sprinkled donuts I already consumed.

Everything is made from scratch at Doe Donuts, which means there's no premixed powders or industrial-sized vats of jam involved. The team cares about what they create, and by selecting two charities each month to donate to, that level of social responsibility extends to the community as well.

FORTUNE

→ **614 SW 11TH AVENUE**
PORTLAND, OR 97205

Fortune hosts a throbbing dance party most nights of the week, but the nightclub is also home to Plant Based Papi, whose vegan menus have been popping up around town for the past few years. Now, Papi has found a permanent home at Fortune, located inside Portland's Sentinel Hotel.

The man behind the menu, Jewan Manuel (aka the Plant-Based Papi), is a pillar of progress for the vegan food movement. It's a dining scene that is often associated with bougie white women who wear Lululemon activewear they never work out in and buy $16 green smoothies from Erewhon. But people of color are chronically underrepresented, which makes no sense because statistically, 8% of African Americans identify as vegetarian or vegan (as opposed to only 3% of the general population).

Don't come here for the dancing; come for the crispy calamari made from mixed-battered mushrooms and served with tartare, house cocktail sauce, and lemon slices. Or try the In-N-Out-style burgers, wedge salad, nachos, and tacos. There's also a fortune teller on site every Friday night from 6 p.m. to 9 p.m. because ... well, why not?

Plant Based Papi's food is also available to order online through Toast and Grubhub, which might be a better fit for us millennials who have somewhere to be in the morning.

BOXCAR PIZZA

VEGAN

→ **2701 NE SANDY BOULEVARD
PORTLAND, OR 97232**

Detroit-style pies are a unique foodbeast. They're short and fat and involve 90-degree angles, with a dense crust that reminds me more of a heavily loaded focaccia. Some argue that it's not even pizza. And let's not get started on Chicago deep dish or ham and pineapple combinations. If you already feel yourself getting triggered by pizza blasphemy, turn the page now. For everyone else who appreciates tasty food in all of its manifestations, read on.

First of all, Boxcar Pizza gets some ravingly positive reviews. I always check the online reviews when considering where to dine, but as we all know, reviews are easily manipulated and must always be taken with some degree of skepticism. In this case, even with my Snowden-esque digital spy tactics and cynical mindset, I struggled to find a word of negativity about Boxcar Pizza. They passed the first test.

Menu-wise, we're working with classic flavor combinations like the traditional pepperoni, mozzarella, and red sauce; a bianca topped with ricotta, mozzarella, and parmesan; and a sausage and pepper pie that hits the spot like a freshly delivered Domino's pizza after a few hazy hours spent at Snoop's crib. But the Boxcar crew like to step outside of the pizza box as well. They offer a steak, cilantro, and lime option and a cheeseburger pie with BBQ sauce, bacon, jalapeños, and ranch that will no doubt get traditionalists reeling. But we probably lost them at the word "vegan" anyway.

The meats here are made from seitan and textured vegetable protein (TVP), and the dairy-free cheeses are based on a typical trinity of coconut oil, starch, and flavorings. It's not my favorite choice of ingredients, but here's the thing: when you combine them in pizza format, nobody's going to care. The net outcome is something hot, oozy, and delicious.

The shop is only open for a short window of time on weeknights (4 p.m. to 9 p.m.), but on Saturday and Sunday, they accept orders starting at midday.

THE SUDRA *(see* p. 221)

DOE DONUTS *(see* p. 222)

FORTUNE *(see* p. 224)

THE SUDRA (*see* p. 221)

SAN FRA
SAN FRA
SAN FRA
SAN FRA
SAN FRA

FERRY BUILDING MARKETPLACE
One Ferry Building #50
San Francisco, CA 94111

SUTRO BATHS
1004 Point Lobos Avenue
San Francisco, CA 94121

**MUSEUM OF THE
AFRICAN DIASPORA**
685 Mission Street
San Francisco, CA 94105

**SAN FRANCISCO MUSEUM
OF MODERN ART**
151 Third Street
San Francisco, CA 94103

**CALIFORNIA ACADEMY OF
SCIENCES (GOLDEN GATE PARK)**
55 Music Concourse Drive
San Francisco, CA 94118

You can tell you're in San Francisco (SF) from the airport food alone. Walk into any newsstand or convenience store, and you'll find racks of protein bars, keto snacks, supplements claiming to offer cognitive enhancement, and unnecessarily pretentious bottled water—the diet of any respectable Silicon Valley tech bro (if they even eat food anymore since slamming a few mouthfuls of meal replacement shake is so much more efficient).

Yet for a city that's fueled by tech innovation and inflated income levels, I found it to be surprisingly scant on progressive vegan dining options. Controversial opinion, I know. A few years ago, PETA named it the most vegan-friendly city in the United States. That's partly due to it being one of the first cities to ban the sale of fur in 2019 (following similar initiatives in Berkeley and my own homeground, West Hollywood). In any case, there are certainly pockets of good eating to be found; I just expected there to be more, considering San Francisco's forward-thinking reputation.

An ideal starting point is the centrally located **Ferry Building Marketplace**, a hub of artisan producers, wine merchants, and specialty stores. The main halls are open every day starting at 7 a.m., but a fresh farmers' market also operates outside on Tuesdays, Thursdays, and Saturdays.

If you're into history, the **Sutro Baths** make a compelling trip. Located along the SF coastline, the pools were once part of an enormoussaltwater swimming complex, which was opened in 1896 by entrepreneur and all-round rich dude Adolf Sutro. It was dismantled many moons ago, but the epic relics are still visible and open to the public.

Continuing on the historical theme, there are several museums I'd recommend checking out between meals. The first is the **Museum of the African Diaspora**, which celebrates—and educates folks on—the art and culture of Black communities.

The **San Francisco Museum of Modern Art (SFMOMA)** is home to one of the country's largest collections of contemporary art, which includes pieces by legends like Andy Warhol and Frida Kahlo.

The **California Academy of Sciences** is located at Golden Gate Park, which, incidentally, is even bigger than New York's Central Park and is a tourist destination in itself. The building is incredible; it houses a planetarium, aquarium, and indoor rainforest. The latter is contained beneath a 90-foot diameter dome and houses actual Amazonian flying fish, which I thought were a sci-fi myth until I looked it up and realized they're real (they don't fly like a bird, but they can jump out of the water and breathe air, which is freaky enough).

GREENS RESTAURANT

VEGETARIAN | VEGAN OPTIONS AVAILABLE

→ **2 MARINA BOULEVARD
(FORT MASON CENTER FOR
ARTS & CULTURE, BUILDING A)
SAN FRANCISCO, CA 94123**

This striking venue was built in the 1970s with the help of renowned architect and Zen Buddhist priest Paul Discoe. As per Discoe's signature style, natural wood is the central element of the restaurant's design, with 12 types flowing from the doors to the walls, tables, stairs, and art features. It's like dining in a very fancy treehouse.

When Greens first opened, chef Deborah Madison was championing the overlooked heirloom varieties of vegetables that most people hadn't even heard of before (there's thousands out there, but we only know what's available in grocery stores and farmers' markets). Madison was first in a long line of female chefs who, over the coming years, became leaders in the farm-to-table movement and established the legacy of Greens.

The menu is split into lunch and dinner courses, which each feature dishes that are crisp, clean, and driven by seasonal fruits and vegetables. It's the kind of food that leaves you feeling better than when you arrived. A salad of blossom bluff peaches with watercress, golden balsamic, goat cheese, and toasted almonds is a beautiful balance of sweetness, tartness, saltiness, and crunch. As is the strawberry salad with jicama, carrots, Thai basil, scallions, and sesame seeds. A summer vegetable curry rich with cauliflower, zucchini, haricot verts, red bell peppers, and Hodo tofu is served alongside papaya salad and brown rice and actually makes me feel healthy.

There's not a nacho to be seen here, and after researching over 500 restaurants for this book, I'm quite relieved.

WILDSEED

VEGAN

→ **2000 UNION STREET**
SAN FRANCISCO, CA 94123

Meet Adriano Paganini: Italian chef and builder of restaurant empires. He owns a slew of hospitality concepts, including Beretta, Delarosa, El Techo de Lolinda, Super Duper Burger, and Uno Dos Tacos. Wildseed is his fully plant-based concept, a restaurant designed to help omnis like me cross the chasm into vegan dining.

To create the menu, Adriano collaborated with another chef from his restaurant group that I'm told is "definitely not vegan." That's an important point to make because for any restaurant or food business to succeed in satisfying nonvegan customers (like Wildseed aims to), it needs to understand where their taste buds are, what expectations they have, and the flavor memories that need to be invoked.

Alternative proteins, like Beyond and Impossible meat, get a whirl on the menu in the form of rigatoni bolognese, pizzas, and a BBQ plate (a feast featuring ribs, sausage, cauliflower, porto bello mushroom, green apple slaw, escabeche, and a slathering of smoky sauce). A crispy chicken sandwich features Tindle meat, and "neatballs" made from mushrooms form a flavorful marsala. While all the dishes are vegan, nowhere on the menu does it scream that fact. For me, that's the key to creating an inclusive space that simply gets people eating more plants and reducing their consumption of animal products without them feeling as though they're being lectured or forced to eat their broccoli at the family dinner table.

Whatever you order, be sure to start with the Mexican corn cakes served with cashews, cherry tomatoes, grilled corn, lime, chili, and queso. It's considered one of the menu's greatest hits. And while this is completely out of character for me, I also recommend ordering the low- or zero-alcohol cocktails. Alcohol-free drinks have been growing in popularity and quality for a few years now, and I've got to say, at Wildseed, they absolutely slap.

For that, my liver says thank you.

5 MINUTES WITH

DAN RIEGLER
COFOUNDER OF KARANA

Dan has lived and worked across the US, Southeast Asia, Sub-Saharan Africa, and Europe as a consultant, startup founder, food writer, and, more embarrassingly, a banker (that was a long time ago, though). These days he's the cofounder of KARANA, a company that uses whole-plant ingredients to make sustainable meat alternatives.

→ **Tell us a little bit about jackfruit and how you use it to make delicious "meat."**

Jackfruit is an absolutely amazing crop! It's the largest treeborn fruit in the world, it's perennial, and it's high yielding, which means it grows tons of fruit without having to disturb the soil. It's also a very durable and resilient crop, so it can stand up against climate change and extreme weather and, in turn, provides a steady income stream for farmers.

The natural fibers of jackfruit very closely mimic the structure of meat, which makes it perfect for creating alternatives to animal products, like pulled pork. It's also full of fiber and nutrients, and because we use it in its unripe stage, the sugars of the fruit haven't formed yet, so it's a great low-glycemic ingredient.

→ **Let's say you're looking to impress some investors in SF. Where are you taking them to lunch?**

Wildseed is always a classic vegan spot with a great menu that highlights both the creativity of using plants as plants and as plant-based meats (including KARANA jackfruit on their spicy sausage pizza!). It's a great showcase of the range and versatility required in plant-based cuisine to drive real adoption and change.

→ **In your opinion, which US city has the best plant-forward food scene? Any gems you're willing to share?**

I have grown to really appreciate the LA food scene recently. It's amazing how extensive the vegan offerings are and how frequently plant-based proteins are showing up on mainstream restaurant menus.

My ideal LA itinerary would include a meal at a great vegan restaurant like **Little Pine** in Silver Lake; their menu changes regularly and is always delicious (the apple sandwich and cookies are personal favorites). Thai food is also excellent in LA; I always end up at **Noree Thai** in West Hollywood, where pretty much anything on the menu can be made vegan. I've spent a lot of time in Thailand and Southeast Asia, and their flavors always take me right back. I love the tofu larb and the stir-fried spicy basil with pumpkin, eggplant, and tofu.

I don't think an LA food trip would be complete without experiencing the awesome pop-up scene. **Jewel** has vegan pop-ups every Monday; I went to a Caribbean dinner there that featured the team from Bridgetown Roti, and it was incredible. Then there's **Melody Wine Bar**, where they have incredible natural wines and bring in great chefs from all over the city for special events.

WILDSEED
See p. 233

LITTLE PINE
2870 Rowena Avenue
Los Angeles, CA 90039

NOREE THAI
7669 Beverly Boulevard
Los Angeles, CA 90036

JEWEL
654 N Hoover Street
Los Angeles, CA 90004

MELODY WINE BAR
751 N Virgil Avenue
Los Angeles, CA 90029

KARANA (*see* p. 234)

GREENS RESTAURANT (*see* p. 232)

LIONS DANCE (*see* p. 238)

LION DANCE CAFE

VEGAN

→ **380 17TH STREET
OAKLAND (OHLONE LAND), CA 94612**

The pandemic was a time when the meek were separated from the wildly opportunistic. Those who played it safe and refused to adapt were first to go; cafes closed, staff was let go, and dining rooms were packed up and left to collect dust. It wasn't always a choice, but the businesses that did survive were often the ones willing to make a drastic pivot or take a big risk.

For others, what was arguably the most devastating economic collapse in recent history felt like an excellent moment to open a restaurant. This was definitely the case for Chefs CY Chia and Shane Stanbridge, formerly of pop-up S+M Vegan.

Funded by a Kickstarter collective of furiously supportive fans, the pair opened their brick-and-mortar dining concept—Lion Dance Cafe—in September 2020, at a time when many of us were still wondering when we'd be allowed to eat together again. They came ready for the virus crisis with a menu of hearty Teochew Singaporean family recipes and hawker dishes, all transport-friendly and ready for takeout.

While there's no dine-in available, there's plenty of prime picnic space at Lake Merritt down the road if you can't wait to get your food home. Be sure to order extra snacks to warm up your palate during transit: maybe a mushroom goreng plump with fried maitake and cut with a preserved lemon sambal, or brined and breaded Hodo tofu nuggets with sambal mayo and curry leaf pickles (this happened to be one of *SF Chronicle*'s top rated dishes of 2020).

For now, the selection of mains is short, but it's frequently changing. Expect a couple of curry and noodle options or a sandwich featuring fried tofu, peanut sauce, cilantro, mayo, and cucumber (a bit like a Singaporean banh mi). The pandan butter nian gao calls to me the most. Traditionally served as a celebratory cake for Chinese New Year, these sweet, sticky mounds are made from rice flour and have the same chewy texture as mochi.

SHIZEN VEGAN SUSHI BAR AND IZAKAYA

VEGAN

→ **370 14TH STREET
SAN FRANCISCO, CA 94103**

Long before *Seaspiracy* came out, Chef Kin Lui was obsessed with ocean life and figuring out how to protect these endangered creatures while still preserving the philosophy of good sushi (remember: sushi is all about vinegared rice, not fish). So when the owners behind Tataki Sushi and Sake Bar—the first sustainable sushi restaurant in the US—decided to take their efforts toward true ocean conservation a step further, Kin Lui was ready.

The starters menu is a safe zone, with edamame, miso soup, and vegetable dumplings—a little familiarity to get you comfortable. But as the menu progresses, dishes become more intriguing and nuanced, broken down into categories based on cooking preparation, such as grilled, braised, and fried (tempura) vegetables.

The reason to come to Shizen, however, is the sushi. Notably, there's been no attempt made to appease people with faux fish; the sushi menu revolves around expertly prepared vegetables and pickling methods, utilizing ingredients such as asparagus, eggplant, peppers, mango, and shitake mushroom. Tofu is the go-to protein and appears in smoked, sweet, spicy, and shredded formats.

For drinks, there's a handful of wine options, but if I were you, I'd explore the sake and shochu collection. That's what they're known for.

Seattle is best known for its seafood, Asian cuisine, and traditional American fare. Fine-dining and health retreats aren't so high on the priority list here, with the population's palate leaning more toward burgers, hot dogs, and pizzas. But given the city's culinary diversity, you'll still find it easy to navigate an animal-free menu among its casual dive bars, coffee houses, and food trucks.

First stop is **Pike Place Market**, where farmers, crafters, and small businesses sell their wares across a nine-acre stretch of downtown real estate. It's open every day of the year, and you can pick up fresh produce starting at 7 a.m. Pike's Place is also where you'll find America's first Starbucks location, which, to this day, attracts hordes of tourists. Step in line at your own peril; it moves quickly, but it can be a frustrating wait for those who haven't had their morning coffee.

If you're traveling on a budget, try foraging for free at the **Beacon Food Forest**. Located on public parkland and maintained by a dedicated group of volunteers, the forest is a self-contained ecosystem of fruits, vegetables, herbs, and other edible plants. Anyone is welcome to a DIY harvest—just bring a reusable bag and be sure to take only what you need, leaving the rest for others to enjoy.

For cultural enrichment, be sure to check out **Ada's Technical Books and Cafe**, which features a vegetarian menu and coworking space. It's known for catering to very specific tastes, both culinary and literary, and is the first place I'd recommend to any tourist seeking a feminist science-fiction book subscription.

Another must-see is the **Museum of Pop Culture (MoPOP)**. Designed to resemble a smashed guitar, the building is unmissable, but if you need a further visual guide, it's located next door to the iconic Space Needle.

The exhibits at MoPOP are constantly evolving. There's an entire collection dedicated to the history of hip-hop, a showcase of Disney costumes, and the Science Fiction Hall of Fame. If you're lucky, you might also catch a glimpse of Kurt Cobain's original Fender Stratocaster. Incidental trivia that I know from teenage years spent obsessively listening to Nirvana: Cobain grew up in Seattle and was a vegetarian.

PIKE PLACE MARKET
85 Pike Street
Seattle, WA 98101

BEACON FOOD FOREST
North Beacon Hill (adjacent to Jefferson Park at 16th Avenue S and S Dakota Street)

ADA'S TECHNICAL BOOKS AND CAFE
425 15th Avenue E
Seattle, WA 98112

MUSEUM OF POP CULTURE (MOPOP)
325 Fifth Avenue N
Seattle, WA 98109

FRANKIE & JO'S

VEGAN | WOMAN-OWNED

→ **1010 E UNION STREET**
   SEATTLE, WA 98122

→ **1411 NW 70TH STREET**
   SEATTLE, WA 98117

→ **4619 VILLAGE TERRACE DRIVE NE**
   SEATTLE, WA 98105

Nobody ever complains about vegan ice cream like they do about meat or cheese alternatives. If it's sweet and creamy, it's going to hit the spot regardless of the ingredients.

At Frankie & Jo's, they're replacing the traditional dairy and whey protein situation with coconut and oat milks to create icy-cold confections. The original scoop shop, which boasts a modern, light-filled space adorned with fern wallpaper, opened in the Capitol Hill neighborhood back in 2016. Since then, it's expanded to three locations, the latest opening its doors in University Village (just look for the peach-hued shopfront; you can't miss it).

As a certified B Corporation, Frankie & Jo's is committed to being more than a guilty treat. Not only is the menu fully plant-based, but it's created around sustainable supply chain practices and real, natural ingredients. Many of the flavors are sweetened exclusively with whole foods or alternative sugars, such as Medjool dates, maple syrup, and coconut sugar, and they don't rely on added gums or stabilizers like commercial ice creams frequently do.

Flavors change monthly here but might include salty lime and watermelon, tahini banana, pineapple whip, salty caramel ash, golden milk, and beet strawberry rose, available by the cup or cone. I highly recommend trying out the latter; the maple-vanilla waffle cones are sugar-free and made from flax seed and oat flour, which gives them a little more heft and crunch than the traditional, brittle supermarket cone variety.

If you can't make it to a F&J location, you can score a pint at Whole Foods, Jimbo's, and Erewhon.

CYCLE DOGS

VEGAN

→ **5410 17TH AVENUE NW
SEATTLE, WA 98107**

As someone who spent a dreary seven years working in the bowels of government, I get how the standard nine-to-five doesn't always equate to living your best life. I mean, I ditched that comfortable salary to become a plant-based cheese mogul and live a life of feverish insecurity as a startup founder. So the fact that Keaton Tucker left an architectural firm to pursue his passions and open Seattle's first all-vegan hot dog stop makes complete sense to me. Some of us are just hardwired to be entrepreneurs.

Keaton started Cycle Dogs as a one-man show, with a hot dog cart powered by a bicycle. The menu was small, but a loyal following grew, and by year two, he was ready to scale up to a food truck, allowing the business to cover more ground and offer a more extensive menu.

A successful Kickstarter campaign, which raised $50,000 from a whopping 490 public backers, allowed the Cycle Dogs team to open a permanent home in Seattle's Ballard neighborhood in 2021. Since then, the menu has expanded further, introducing burgers, Caesar salad bowls, and plates of buttery street corn licked with lime and cayenne. There's also a weekend brunch menu that includes burritos and breakfast sandwiches. Go if you like tofu. If you don't, the Beyond breakfast sausage will satisfy those protein cravings.

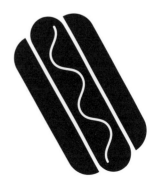

FLYING APRON

VEGAN | GLUTEN-FREE

→ **4709 CALIFORNIA AVENUE SW
SEATTLE, WA 98116**

Flying Apron is a safe room for the gluten intolerant. You will not be judged here for menu modifications and pesky dietary requests, nor will you need to pull out your mobile lab testing kit to check the pizza dough for signs of wheat. Even for a vegan venue, this freedom is hard to come by.

The menu here is constantly changing, which is partly a reflection of their commitment to fresh and local ingredients, but also to keep things interesting. It's built on a backbone of hot dishes, like lasagna with made-from-scratch cashew-based cheese, soups, salads, gluten-free beverages (including beer), and baked goods.

In the sweets department, they offer a variety of cupcakes, cookies, donuts, and cakes by the slice that are made with nonchemical sweeteners instead of refined sugar. That might mean organic agave, maple syrup, or evaporated cane juice. Savory items are made from alternative flour, including brown rice, potato starch, sorghum, millet, and buckwheat. To find out exactly what's baking that day, check their Instagram @flyingapron.

Allergy-friendly celebrations are the real niche that Flying Apron plays to. They regularly host kids' birthday parties and offer customizable packages that include donuts, cupcakes, or even art activities, like designing custom aprons.

GEORGETOWN LIQUOR COMPANY

VEGAN

→ **5501 AIRPORT WAY S, SUITE B
SEATTLE, WA 98108**

In my 20s, I lived across the street from a popular dive bar in Melbourne's Central Business District. I'd teeter precariously across the cobblestones in thoroughly impractical footwear to reach it, sidestepping empty beer cans and spilled McDonald's milkshakes along the way. At the end of the alley and behind the dumpsters was an unmarked open doorway that led to a set of potentially lethal broken stairs. After surviving the climb, I'd land in a dark room lined with band posters and booze bottles. There was always a floorboard or two missing, and Jay-Z's "99 Problems" was somehow always playing over the crackling speakers.

Each week, I'd bring another Tinder date there—perhaps multiple if I'd played my cards right—and order my standard rum with Diet Coke. The bartenders always had my back; they'd pretend they'd never seen me before, let alone my previous succession of dates. It was a quiet understanding that we had. I'd pay them off with a few extra rounds of bourbon at the end of the night.

Everyone needs a solid local dive bar like that in their life, a bar where everybody knows their name. And if I'd lived in Seattle at the time, Georgetown Liquor Company (GLC) probably would have been mine.

GLC knows what it stands for, and that's inclusivity. You won't be accosted by marauding groups of frat bros or receive questionable glances as you parade around in your favorite sequined leotard. This is a space that welcomes alternative culture and individual expression. Also cocktails.

The drinks are straightforward and satisfying and feature far better names than what you might typically expect in a bar of this nature; Reign in Blood is a bloody Mary mix of tomato juice, garlic, basil, and peppercorn-infused vodka, and the Pussy Riot is a simple blend of ginger-infused vodka, muddled lime, and soda.

If you're in for a few rounds of drinks, be sure it's not on an empty stomach. There's a full vegan menu of bar snacks and sandwiches here, and everything—including the seitan meats, cheeses, and sauces—is made in-house.

NOT YOUR EVERYDAY DELI

Vegan cheese and meat is a controversial concept. In Europe, they've managed to ban companies from even labeling their products as such (even going so far as to ban the terms *cheese alternative* and *meat substitute*). But that's a story for another time. Fortunately, the authorities are a little more rational in the US, which means plant-forward charcuterie and fromage lovers have the freedom to use words that most people actually recognize.

BE-HIVE DELI & MARKET

VEGAN

→ **2414 GALLATIN AVENUE**
NASHVILLE, TN 37206

Imagine a crew of band members/housemates who, in between jam sessions, regularly throw vegan potlucks at their pad. That's a party I want to be invited to. And that's exactly how BE-Hive Deli & Market began.

Over the years, more and more people joined these events, and eventually, what started out as a small community collective evolved into a food business. These days, the BE-Hive team has a retail product line of vegan deli meats and sausage, as well as a permanent deli in East Nashville where they serve hot baguettes, cheesesteaks, tacos, fried chicken, and potato tots.

I hope the parties are still running. If they're reading this now, I'd love an invite.

THE VREAMERY

VEGAN

→ **PASO MARKET WALK
1803 SPRING STREET
PASO ROBLES, CA 93446**

Vegan cheese is not typically known for its exceptional melting qualities, but The Vreamery owner Jennifer Golden was determined to prove naysayers wrong with her melt shop, which sells artisan, dairy-free cheeses alongside paninis, bagels, and grazing boxes. Find her at San Luis Obispo area farmers' markets and grab a sandwich straight off the press.

THE HERBIVOROUS BUTCHER

VEGAN

→ **507 FIRST AVENUE NE
MINNEAPOLIS, MN 55413**

Siblings Aubry and Kale Walch, who could very easily be mistaken for the gallery owners of an underground arts collective, have channeled their compassion for animals into a smart business model. At The Herbivorous Butcher, they sell house-made cheeses and meats, snacks, and prepared foods, such as dips and sandwiches, to those who want the traditional deli experience without the animal cruelty.

In 2016, the duo opened their own nonprofit farm sanctuary, Herbivorous Acres, to complement the mission.

THE HERBIVOROUS BUTCHER

THE HERBIVOROUS BUTCHER

RIVERDEL

REBEL CHEESE

VEGAN

→ **2200 ALDRICH STREET, SUITE 120
AUSTIN, TX 78723**

Kirsten Maitland and Fred Zwar had a dream to create vegan-friendly picnics, and this store is the embodiment of that wish, a place to source small-batch cheeses, charcuterie, jams and chutneys, pickles, and crackers for the perfect plant-based picnic platter. The cheeses are nut-based (cashew or almond), and if you're too hungry to wait, you can order a soup and sandwich and dine in.

RIVERDEL

VEGAN

→ **ESSEX MARKET
88 ESSEX STREET
NEW YORK, NY 10002**

This is my favorite plant-based cheesery, mainly because the owner, Michaela, was one of our earliest supporters when we moved to the US to launch Grounded. I remember taking a box of samples—our very first prototypes—and getting her feedback. She commented that some of the flavor profiles were very much for the "European palate," and we immediately understood what she meant. If you've ever eaten cheese outside of the States, you'll know what she meant as well. In any case, Michaela knows her stuff.

Her stall at New York's Essex Market is laid out like any other deli cheese counter. It's not until you get up close that you realize nothing contains dairy. There's big, bloomy blocks of washed-rind cheese and artisan wheels cut to order. You'll also find a small range of packaged products and a strong focus on local suppliers. If you can't make it to NYC, you can hop online and order direct (Riverdel ships nationwide, riverdelcheese.com).

MELLOW MUSHROOM

VEGAN OPTIONS AVAILABLE

→ **FOR LOCATIONS, VISIT MELLOWMUSHROOM.COM.**

Mellow Mushroom has a dedicated menu of animal-free and gluten-free options, and while they're by no means the only pizza chain offering plant-based alternatives, their branding resembles an early '90s Nickelodeon acid trip, so they felt worthy of inclusion here.

According to Mellow Mushroom and their legion of fans, pizza is a pretty spiritual experience. Here, it becomes elevated with hand-tossed, stone-baked dough made from unbleached flour; slow-simmered, preservative-free sauce; and a range of plant-based toppings to decorate your crust, including soy-free vegan cheese and tempeh. In addition to the pizzas, there's a short vegan menu of salads, hoagies, calzones, sweets, and most importantly, a build-your-own option for those with sensitive tummies.

Mellow Mushroom also claims to have "the greenest pizza box in the country," which is made from 100% recycled materials and boasts a negative carbon footprint. Can Domino's match that commitment? We'll wait.

NATIVE FOODS

VEGAN

→ FOR LOCATIONS, VISIT NATIVEFOODS.COM.

Native Foods is one of the OG Californian restaurants to bring ethical and earth-friendly options into the mainstream. Bear in mind that 1994 was a very different time: people were watching episodes of *Seinfeld* and *Friends* for the first time, and soy was the only alternative milk available at the grocery store. But Native Foods stuck it out and has since grown into a national chain, with its mission being to feed us convenient but wholesome, non-GMO meals.

The menu reads like that of a typical casual restaurant chain: stacks of burgers and sandwiches that can be ordered in a combo along with sides, like fries, salad, soup, or even steamed kale. It's a nonthreatening way to introduce the meat-free concept to the mainstream. Without knowing it was vegan, I bet very few people would turn down the bumper burger, which is loaded with sliced brisket, fried onion rings, provolone, Southern slaw, and pickle chips inside a toasted pretzel bun.

TIP

Come Thanksgiving, you can order take-home feasts that feature a family-sized Wellington and sides for only $60. How they manage to provide that much food at such a low price, I don't know, but I'm not complaining.

VOODOO DOUGHNUT

VEGAN OPTIONS AVAILABLE

→ **VIEW LOCATIONS AT VOODOODOUGHNUT.COM.**

So this one's a cracker: a chain of donut stores founded by an eccentric duo of entertainers who have created a business model around unconventional and creative, fried dough rings.

Voodoo Doughnut, which has locations in Texas, Oregon, California, Colorado, and Florida, channels some serious *Beetlejuice* energy. There's music blaring, ostentatious chandeliers overhead, and hot-pink walls lined with miniature coffins and Burton-esque dream creatures. At first glance, it looks more like an alternative music store or punk clothing brand. The fast food–style counter and Insta-worthy donut display is the only reminder that you are indeed at the right place.

The menu has my blood sugar spiking just by looking at it, yet I lack the willpower to walk away from a raspberry jelly donut coated in chocolate frosting and stabbed with a pretzel stick. There's a donut with eyes and a mustache (made with innards of maple and Bavarian cream) and one that comes packed with peanut butter and jelly, like a school lunch. Personally, I like the donut that's dusted with cinnamon and shaped like a fat blunt and the Diablos Rex, a chunky chocolate cake–style donut with a vanilla-flavored pentagram iced on top. Note that the last two are not typically made vegan but can be if you order ahead.

SIDE NOTE

All locations offer legal wedding ceremonies.

MAYA'S COOKIES

VEGAN | WOMAN-OWNED

→ **4760 MISSION GORGE PLACE, SUITE G SAN DIEGO, CA 92120**

→ **250 NORTH CITY DRIVE, SUITE 8**

→ **SAN MARCOS, CA 92078**

Founded by bad-ass female entrepreneur Maya Madsen, this Black-owned cookie powerhouse has been pumping out vegan treats since 2015. They're doing all the favorites, like birthday cake, s'mores, double chocolate chunk, and snickerdoodle, as well as gluten-free varieties. It's like a vegan F-you to Mrs. Field's—and even omnis find it compelling.

If you can't swing a visit to the brick-and-mortar stores, all is not lost; Maya delivers her cookies nationwide. Having tested them through the gauntlet of USPS, we can confirm that they hold up to transport well. However, once tasted, they're probably not going to last long, so consider the monthly subscription service to keep your kitchen stocked with sweets.

MAYAS COOKIES (*see* p. 259)

(*see* p. 259)

MELLOW MUSHROOM (*see* p. 256)

VOODOO DOUGHNUTS (*see* p. 258)

PES
PES
PES
PES
PES

My husband, Shaun, is an incredibly talented chef. I tease him constantly for his predilection toward making what I call "art food" (others might call it molecular gastronomy; he just calls it cooking), his fancy awards, and his arm tattoos, which seem to be a requirement for anyone working in a kitchen. We met in 2015, in the same week he opened his first solo fine-dining restaurant in Melbourne, Australia.

It was a multisensory concept that went beyond the spectrum of flavor alone, aiming to ignite all of the senses through sound, smell, and touch. There were sound and lighting engineers involved, live actors and musicians secretly placed within the room to steer the diner's journey, and the incorporation of 3D printing and augmented reality. And the set menu stretched a ridiculous 16 courses over several hours. Somehow, it never felt tiring, only exciting, as guests wondered what was about to happen next.

The dishes were spectacular: a lemon meringue pie shaped into life-sized lemons hanging from an edible tree, nougat made from upcycled fish scales, oysters made from celeriac, and a chocolate ganache cake made from lamb's blood (obviously this was not a vegan restaurant). Out of all of these fantastical courses, it struck me as odd that Shaun started serving such a boring cheese course at the end of the meal.

It was a simple wedge of Gruyere. A tiny wheel of Camembert. A slice of blue cheese. All tasty, of course, just not in keeping with the creativity of his menu.

At least, that's what I thought until the day he told me that the cheeses were not dairy after all. They were, in fact, made from hemp. I should've known by that point that nothing Shaun does is ever as simple as it seems.

I went home that night with an idea for a food company, one that actually made plant-based cheese taste like ... cheese. Something so delicious and sexy that everyday people would be happy to eat it in place of dairy cheese any day of the week with zero sense of compromise and no crazy price tag. That's how the concept of Grounded Foods Co. was born.

Over the coming weeks, I argued my case to Shaun that this was a massive opportunity. "Plant-based cheese is going to be huge. I need you to quit this career you've spent the past 20 years building and let me hire you as my R+D chef. We'll bring hemp cheese to the world!"

I'm grateful that Shaun trusted me on this one because within a few weeks, we'd secured our first venture capital investment, had completely walked away from the restaurant and our former lives in Australia, said goodbye to friends and family, and moved to the United States to launch Grounded Foods Co. That's the moment you found me at the beginning of this book.

Shortly after we left our former restaurant, the entire hospitality industry crashed. COVID-19 cut through the food community with ruthless vengeance, affecting everyone from restaurant owners and their staff to the family-run suppliers who no longer had customers to sell their produce to. It felt like we'd stepped out of the way of a car crash just moments before the collision.

Now, Shaun and I spend our days building Grounded Foods Co., a company that makes wildly innovative plant-based cheeses from hemp seed. We launched into Whole Foods last year and, within months, had spread into 1000 stores across the country. All our cheeses are animal-free, nut-free, soy-free, gluten-free, non-GMO, and keto. But most importantly, they're made by a very good chef who believes in flavor first.

While he doesn't get the opportunity to make 16-course meals anymore, he's still blowing people's minds with food that's more than meets the eye. Here are some of the recipes he created for those of us playing along at home.

FOCACCIA WITH HEMP SEED GOAT CHEESE, CHERRY TOMATOES, AND PEPPERS (see p. 271)

ASPARAGUS TART WITH HEMP SEED CREAM CHEESE

SERVES 4

1 sheet vegan puff pastry, thawed

8 oz Grounded hemp seed cream cheese, onion + chive flavor

2 bunches asparagus, woody stalks removed

Salt and pepper to taste

1 tbsp olive oil

Zest of 1 lemon

Preheat the oven to 350°F. Line a baking sheet with parchment paper.

Place pastry onto the lined baking sheet. Using a knife, score a 1-inch border around the edges, being careful not to cut all the way through.

Spread the cream cheese onto the puff pastry, staying within the borders. Lay whole spears of asparagus on top of the pastry and season with salt and pepper. Brush the edges of the pastry with olive oil and drizzle a little on top of the asparagus for good measure.

Bake in the oven for 15 minutes (or until the pastry is crispy and cooked in the middle).

Remove from the oven and top with lemon zest. Allow to cool before serving

BEAST MODE FRIES

A PLANT-BASED REPLICA OF ONE OF LA'S MOST POPULAR SECRET MENU ITEMS

SERVES 4

1 bag of frozen fries

1 tbsp olive oil

1 large yellow onion, thinly sliced

½ tsp salt

1 tsp brown sugar

3 tbsp vegan mayo

1 tbsp ketchup

1 tbsp sweet pickle relish

½ tsp white vinegar

½ pouch of Grounded CHEESE FREE CHEESE squeeze - American Style

Preheat the oven to 350°F. Cook frozen fries as per package instructions.

While the fries are baking, heat olive oil in a skillet and add the sliced onion, salt, and brown sugar. Stir frequently until thick and caramelized.

To make the dressing, mix together the mayo, ketchup, pickle relish, and vinegar in a small bowl.

To serve, transfer fries into a serving dish. Top with caramelized onion, creamy dressing, and lashings of Grounded CHEESE FREE CHEESE squeeze. Enjoy.

CYPRIOT GRAIN SALAD

SERVES 4

1 cup freekeh

½ cup Puy lentils

1 bunch cilantro, chopped

½ bunch parsley, chopped

½ red onion, finely diced

2 tbsp toasted pumpkin seeds

2 tbsp toasted slivered almonds

2 tbsp toasted pine nuts

2 tbsp baby capers

½ cup currants

Seeds of 1 pomegranate

1 tsp cumin seeds, toasted
and ground

1 tbsp agave syrup
(or vegan honey)

Juice of ½ lemon

8 oz Grounded marinated hemp
seed goat cheese (reserve
marinade for the dressing)

Sea salt to taste

Blanch freekeh and lentils separately in boiling water until al dente. Drain well and allow to cool.

In a medium bowl, combine the cilantro, parsley, red onion, toasted seeds, nuts, capers, currants, and pomegranate. Add the cooked freekeh and lentils.

To make the dressing, combine the ground cumin, agave, lemon juice, and goat cheese marinade and stir well. Season to taste.

Add dressing to the salad mixture and toss. Top with Grounded marinated hemp seed goat cheese and serve immediately.

NOTE

Freekeh is used as the base in this salad, but you can make it gluten-free by substituting it with quinoa, buckwheat, or brown rice.

GREEN BEAN, CRANBERRY, AND GOAT CHEESE SALAD

SERVES 4

2 tsp olive oil

1 lb green beans, trimmed

⅓ cup blanched slivered almonds

⅓ cup dried cranberries

4 oz Grounded hemp seed goat cheese, cut into small cubes

DRESSING

3 tbsp olive oil

1 tbsp red wine vinegar

1 garlic clove, minced

Heat a cast-iron skillet over medium-high heat. Add the oil, and when hot, add the beans. Let them blister for about 90 seconds, then toss and allow to blister for another 60 seconds. Remove from heat and transfer to a large serving bowl.

In a small pan, toast the almonds by stirring over high heat for 2 minutes or until browned (no oil needed). Set aside.

For the dressing, whisk ingredients together in a small bowl (or place in an empty jar and shake to combine).

Add cranberries, Grounded hemp seed goat cheese, toasted almonds, and dressing to the bowl with green beans. Toss together and serve.

NOTE

You can substitute the marinade from the goat cheese for olive oil in this recipe.

TRUFFLED MAC + CHEESE

SERVES 6

2 tbsp plant-based butter
(plus extra to butter the
baking dish)

1 lb macaroni

8 oz pouch Grounded
CHEESE FREE CHEESE squeeze

2 tsp truffle oil

¾ cup breadcrumbs

2 tbsp fresh herbs
(parsley, thyme, chives,
and/or rosemary)

Salt and pepper to taste

Preheat the oven to 350°F. Generously butter a shallow
2-quart baking dish.

Cook the macaroni in a large pot of boiling salted water
until al dente. Drain, reserving about a ½ cup of the cooking
liquid. Return the macaroni to the pot.

Add the Grounded CHEESE FREE CHEESE squeeze and truffle
oil to the macaroni and stir well to combine. If necessary,
use a splash of the cooking liquid to thin it out so the pasta
is completely covered in cheese sauce. Spread the macaroni
into the prepared baking dish.

In a small microwave-safe bowl, melt the remaining butter.
Add the breadcrumbs and herbs to the bowl and season
with salt and pepper. Stir well to combine.

Sprinkle the breadcrumb mixture evenly over the macaroni.
Bake in the oven for 30 minutes or until browned and
bubbling. Serve warm.

FOCACCIA WITH HEMP SEED GOAT CHEESE, CHERRY TOMATOES, AND PEPPERS

SERVES 8

FOCACCIA DOUGH

Neutral oil, for greasing

1¾ cups room-temperature water

¼ cup non-dairy milk

1 tsp sugar

2½ tsp instant dry yeast

4½ cups all-purpose flour

1½ tsp salt

Marinade from 1 tub of Grounded hemp seed goat cheese (reserve cheese for focaccia topping)

TOPPINGS

½ red pepper, finely diced

½ yellow pepper, finely diced

½ cup cherry tomatoes, halved

2 garlic cloves, finely minced

1 tbsp fresh rosemary, chopped

½ red onion, sliced

Handful of fresh basil

Sea salt

1 bunch fresh chives

8 oz Grounded hemp seed goat cheese

Oil a large bowl and set aside. To make the dough, combine the water, milk, sugar, and yeast in a large bowl and mix. Leave for 5 minutes until it's foamy.

Add the flour, salt, and goat cheese marinade and begin mixing with a wooden spoon (or use a counter top mixer with a dough hook on medium speed). Knead until smooth and glossy (about 8 minutes). Add more flour if needed to stop the dough from sticking.

Next, transfer the dough to a large oiled bowl. Cover with plastic wrap and leave in a warm place to rise until the dough has doubled in size (about 1 hour).

Preheat the oven to 425°F. Line a medium-sized baking tin with parchment paper and press the dough firmly into the tin. Cover with plastic wrap and leave for another 30 minutes to rise.

Remove plastic wrap and press small dents into the dough with your thumbs (aim to create about 12 little pools). In an alternating fashion, fill each dent with a mound of diced pepper or a slice of cherry tomato.

Sprinkle the garlic, rosemary, onion, basil leaves, and sea salt onto the dough.

Lay the sprigs of chive on top and bake in the preheated oven for 25 minutes.

Remove from the oven and leave to cool for 5 minutes before flipping the focaccia out of its tin (keep the toppings facing up).

Finally, add dots of the Grounded hemp seed goat cheese. Cut into wedges and serve warm.

FOCACCIA WITH HEMP SEED GOAT CHEESE, CHERRY TOMATOES, AND PEPPERS (*see* p. 271)

CYPRIOT GRAIN SALAD (*see* p. 268)

**ASPARAGUS TART WITH HEMP SEED
CREAM CHEESE** (*see* p. 266)

ABOUT
THE AUTHOR

Veronica Fil is an Australian writer, foodtech entrepreneur and the co-founder of Grounded Foods Co.—a startup making hemp-based dairy alternatives. She currently lives in Los Angeles with her husband Shaun and tiny poodle Archie, and spends far too much time on TikTok talking about plant-based food (@groundedcfc).

CONTRIBUTORS

Chloe Mendel

Dan Riegler

Michael Fox

Elysabeth Alfano

Kirsten Sutaria

Shaun Quade

Laura Ross   Michael Valverde

Cara Woodhouse   Bill Fold

Pete LaCombe   Tara Punzone

Gigi Jones   Carmen Santillan

INDEX

PHOTO CREDITS

Thank you to all who provided photos for this book. Copyright for each image is listed below.

p. 3 – Unsplash/Jaszlyn Brown

p. 4 – Madelynne Boykin

p. 9 – Akin Odebiyi

p. 13 – Unsplash/Megan Bucknall

pp. 18, 22 – Bouldin Creek Café

p. 23 (top) – Tracey Stable/ Rebel Cheese

p. 23 (bottom) – Counter Culture

p. 27 – Unsplash/Oleksandr Baiev

p. 28 – Amitabul

p. 31 – Althea

p. 36 – Liberation Kitchen

p. 39 – Kitchen 17

p. 43 – Unsplash/DJ Johnson

p. 45 – Munch

p. 46 – Cleveland Vegan

pp. 56, 68, 78, 93, 107, 180, 192, 205 – Shutterstock

p. 62 – Portia's Cafe

p. 64 – Alisha Skeel/Pattycake Bakery

p. 72 (top) – Kimberly Jurgens

p. 72 (bottom) – Belse Plant Cuisine

p. 73 – Hari Chan

p. 81 – Chelsea Chorpenning/ Somebody People

p. 86 – Brianna Berry, @ glutenfreekentucky

p. 94 – Chili Mustard Onions

p. 100 – Samantha Jo Photography

p. 103 – Jeremy Damaske

p. 108 – Pirate's Bone Burgers

p. 111 – Jessica Best

p. 114 – Mudpie Bakery & Coffeehouse

pp. 124, 127 – Chikyū Vegan Sushi Bar

p. 126 (top left) – @tarantinosvegan

p. 126 (top right) – Veg-in-Out Market

p. 126 (bottom) – Tacotarian

p. 131 – Unsplash/Towfiqu Barbhuiya

p. 133 – Underground Burger

p. 137 – Unsplash/Izayah Ramos

pp. 139, 158 – Talia Dinwiddie/ Sage Plant Based Bistro

p. 149 – Photos by Oliver Barth

p. 153 – Nic's on Beverly

p. 159 (top) – M Lifson / Shutterstock.com

p. 159 (bottom) – @Beckysbitesrecipes

p. 162 – Unsplash/Guzman Barquin

p. 165 – Planta

p. 166 – Minty Z

p. 172 – Unsplash/Fabien Bazanegue

p. 174 – Beyond Sushi

p. 183 – Eric Medsker/Ladybird

p. 184 – Screamer's Pizzeria

p. 189 – Robert K. Chin - Storefronts / Alamy Stock Photo

p. 194 – Unsplash/Rachael Gorjestani

p. 197 – Dharma Southern Kitchen

p. 201 – Black Bean Deli

p. 209 – HipCityVeg

p. 210 – Bar Bombon

p. 212 – Charlie was a sinner.

p. 218 – Unsplash/Justin Shen

pp. 223, 226 (bottom left) – Doe Donuts

pp. 226 (top), 227 – The Sudra

p. 226 (bottom right) – Christine Dong

p. 230 – Unsplash/Fran

pp. 236 (top) – Karana

pp. 236 (bottom) – Nader Khouri

p. 237 – Ariana Zhang

p. 243 – Unsplash/Joel Mott

p. 244 – Reva Keller

p. 246 – Cycle Dogs

p. 253 – The Herbivorous Butcher

p. 254 – Riverdel

p. 260 – Kinda Arzon Photography @kindaarzonphotography

p. 261 (top) – Thomas Trompeter / Shutterstock.com

p. 261 (bottom) – SvetlanaSF / Shutterstock.com

pp. 265, 266, 267, 269, 270, 272–3 – Veronica Fil/ Grounded

Published in 2023 by Hardie Grant Explore, an imprint of Hardie Grant Publishing

Hardie Grant Explore (Melbourne)
Wurundjeri Country
Building 1, 658 Church Street
Richmond, Victoria 3121

Hardie Grant Explore (Sydney)
Gadigal Country
Level 7, 45 Jones Street
Ultimo, NSW 2007

www.hardiegrant.com/au/explore

All rights reserved. No part of this publication may be reproduced, stored in a retrieval system or transmitted in any form by any means, electronic, mechanical, photocopying, recording or otherwise, without the prior written permission of the publishers and copyright holders.

The moral rights of the author have been asserted.

Copyright text © Veronica Fil 2023
Copyright concept and design
© Hardie Grant Publishing 2023

A catalogue record for this book is available from the National Library of Australia

Hardie Grant acknowledges the Traditional Owners of the Country on which we work, the Wurundjeri People of the Kulin Nation and the Gadigal People of the Eora Nation, and recognises their continuing connection to the land, waters and culture. We pay our respects to their Elders past and present.

For all relevant publications, Hardie Grant Explore commissions a First Nations consultant to review relevant content and provide feedback to ensure suitable language and information is included in the final book. Hardie Grant Explore also includes traditional place names and acknowledges Traditional Owners, where possible, in both the text and mapping for their publications.

Plant-based USA: A travel guide to eating animal-free in America
ISBN 9781741177336

10 9 8 7 6 5 4 3 2 1

Publisher
Melissa Kayser

Project editor
Megan Cuthbert

Editor
Lyric Dodson

Proofreader
Allison Hiew

Design
Evi-O.Studio | Kait Polkinghorne

Typesetting
Megan Ellis

Index
Max McMaster

Production coordinator
Simone Wall

Colour reproduction by Megan Ellis and Splitting Image Colour Studio

Printed and bound in China by LEO Paper Products LTD.

The paper this book is printed on is certified against the Forest Stewardship Council® Standards and other sources. FSC® promotes environmentally responsible, socially beneficial and economically viable management of the world's forests.